The Chessmaster Checklist

Andrew Soltis

T0323188

First published in the United Kingdom in 2021
by B.T. Batsford Ltd
43 Great Ormond Street
London
WC1N 3HZ

ISBN: 9781849947145

A CIP catalogue record for this book is available from the British Library.

25 24 23 22 21
10 9 8 7 6 5 4 3 2 1

Reproduction by Rival Colour, UK
Printed by CPI Mackays, UK

This book can be ordered direct from the publisher at www.pavilionbooks.com, or try your local bookshop

MIX
Paper from
responsible sources
FSC   FSC® C020471
www.fsc.org

Contents

Introduction

"If I move my queen to d5, can it be captured?"

Beginners ask themselves questions like this. They learn the hard way. If they don't ask, they lose a lot of queens.

But even strong players fail to ask.

Daulyte – Socko
Sochi 2015
White to move

No, the diagram is not wrong – 57 b6 is indeed mate.

Yet White played **57 ♕a5+???** and immediately resigned. And this was a world championship event.

Newcomers to chess are shocked by this. How can one of the world's best players make the worst of blunders?

But tournament veterans know how, from personal experience:

You want to make a forcing move. You see the check on a5. You pick up the queen and put it there. You only see 57...♕xa5! when your hand lets go of it.

Beginners learn to protect themselves, in a beginner way. They grab the piece they want to move and place it on the desired square. They know the touch-move rule so they hold it there, often with one finger, until they have scouted the rest of the board to see if the piece can be captured.

It's a clumsy procedure. But even grandmasters have used it – badly.

Morozevich – Svetushkin
European Team Championship 2011
Black to move

White's only real winning chance lies in capturing the b3-pawn and then outplaying Black in a drawable ♔+♖+♗-vs.- ♔+♖ ending.

Of course, he might also win if Black blunders horribly. But Black was not only a grandmaster but an experienced teacher of young players. He taught them the paramount value of rechecking the move you want to play before you make it on the board.

He picked up his rook, placed it on a new square and held it there. He looked about the board and then let go of the rook, **76...♖g2??**.

He resigned immediately after **77 ♖xg2!**.

Chess Adolescence

When you were a beginner you learned to do a lot of things. You probably didn't realize it, but some were things you did subconsciously.

When you decided on a move, you didn't think about how to make it on the board. You didn't ask yourself "Should I slide the piece or pick it up? If I pick it up, should I use two fingers or three? Or all five?"

No, moving a piece had become as natural as any everyday routine, like putting on your shoes.

You learn more good routines in your chess adolescence. After your opponent moves, you wonder "Does he threaten something?"

At first, you had to remind yourself to do that. But as you improve, you look for a threat without prompting. You may do it instantly.

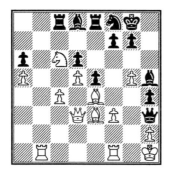

Nakamura – Carlsen
Internet 2020
White to move

When Hikaru Nakamura played **30 &b6**, Magnus Carlsen didn't have to ask himself if there was a threat. He saw 31 &xd8.

But he did not stop there. He also spotted 31 &f5!.

He immediately replied **30...&xg5!**.

He was worse after **31 &f5! &g6! 32 &xh3 &xd3 33 &xc8 &xc8** but managed to draw.

Carlsen knew to look for more than one threat. After all, he was once a chess adolescent, 20 years before.

Habit Building

You get better at chess by acquiring other good habits. You won't get *much* better until you can perform those habits without thinking.

For example, you will not only ask yourself "What does his last move threaten?" but also "What does it allow me to do?"

You may ask specific questions such as "Which of my pieces can I improve" but also general questions such as "What is his weakest point?" and "What is his goal in the next few moves?"

Masters are masters because they ask themselves these and other questions. They form a checklist.

In the heyday of postal chess, many correspondence players used an actual written list of do's and don'ts. Consulting it was their final step before they sent their next move off in the mail.

But you can't comfortably play chess, over the board or on the Internet, by trying to remember these questions. It is awkward, wasteful and often just confusing.

Instead, you should internalize these questions, to use a fancy word:

1 What Does He Threaten?

2 What Are The Tactical Ideas?

3 What Is Wrong With His Move?

4 What Is The Principled Move?

5 What Is His Weakest Point?

6 What Does He Want?

7 How Can I Improve My Pieces?

8 Will My Position Get Better?

9 Is There A Better Move?

10 How Can My Move Be A Blunder?

Asking these questions should become effortless and automatic. It should be as comfortable as ... well, putting on your shoes.

Chapter One:
What Does He Threaten?

This is one of the first questions players learn to ask themselves – and one of the first they forget.

Even grandmasters forget it. They forget because they are busy asking other questions.

Karjakin – Anton Guijarro
Internet 2020
White to move

White understood that Black's best chance for survival lay in perpetual check (46 g4 ♕e2+ 47 ♔g3 ♕e1+).

He met that threat with **46 ♗e3** so that 46...♕e2+ 47 ♗f2.

This defeats all of Black's possible moves – except for the winning **46...♗h3+!**. It was Black's second and stronger threat.

White is either mated (47 ♔f2 ♕f1 mate and 47 ♔h2 ♕f1) or loses his queen (47 ♔xh3 ♕h1+ 48 ♔g4 ♕h5+ 49 ♔f4 g5+ and ...♕xf7).

Sergey Karjakin, who had played a world championship match four years before, was the victim in that game. He was the beneficiary in this one:

Wei Yi – Karjakin
Internet 2020
Black to move

White threatens ♖xc6+. He would win after 38...♘xc5?? 39 ♖xc6+.

He also planned to meet 38...♔d5 with 39 ♖d7+!.

Then he would be winning after 39...♔e6?? 40 ♖xd3 or 39...♔c4 40 ♖d4+! and ♖xh4.

So, when Karjakin moved **38...♔f5**, White didn't have to ask "Why?" He had figured out that it was the only safe Black move.

White replied **39 ♖f7+.** His idea was to meet 39...♔e5 with 40 ♖h7 and ♖xh4.

Karjakin chose **39...♔g6** and the position was repeated after **40 ♖c7!** **♔f5.**

White to move

Of course, White can continue 41 ♖f7+. But even with only seconds left he wanted more than a draw by repetition.

He was careful enough to look for a trap. He spotted one: 41 ♖xc6 would lose to 41...♘e5+.

He set his own trap with **41 ♖h7**. Then 41...♘xc5? would lose a piece to 42 ♖h5+.

But the game ended with **41...♘e1 mate**!.

10

Wrong Question

In your chess adolescence you asked "What is his threat?" after your opponent moved. You learned to do this instinctively. But this is the wrong question.

It is wrong because once you spot an opponent's threat you may let your guard down. This is what White did when he saw 41 ♖xc6? ♘e5+. He didn't look for another tactic, the mating threat.

Players are particularly vulnerable to this pitfall when they see more than one way to avert a threat. They focus on finding the best defense to it. Once they feel they have found it, they think their work is done.

Ding Liren – Nakamura
Internet 2020
White to move

White saw the threat of 28...♕e4+ followed by 29 ♕xe4 fxe4+ and 30....♖xd5.

He can avert that in several ways:

He can trade rooks, 28 ♖xd8.

That would work well after 28...♖xd8 29 ♗b6 ♖e8 30 ♕d5! – but less so after 29...♖d7.

Alternatively, he can move his king out of checking range. But 28 ♔e2 gets into a pin that Black can try to exploit with 28...♗h6, or 28...b5 first.

There is also a benefit – but also a drawback – to putting one of his rooks on d2.

In the end, White chose **28 ♔g2**.

Black to move

It had none of the drawbacks of the alternatives and one major benefit.

The ♗b6 idea is stronger. For example, 29 ♗b6! ♖c8? 30 ♕xc8 or 29...♖xd5 30 ♕xd5 and ♖c7.

But 28 ♔g2?? was a blunder. White forgot to look for a second threat.

He resigned after **28...b5! 29 ♕b3 ♕b7!** cost him a rook.

Near Term

"What is his threat?" is the wrong question. The right one is "What does he threaten?" The answer may be a plural.

When there is more than one threat, there are two very different ways to blunder.

A young player will see the obvious threat, such as a threat to mate next move. But he may not detect a long-term threat, such as to win a piece in two or three moves.

Experienced players develop a sense of danger that often alerts them to a long-term threat. But this foresight can work against them. It can blind them to a near-term threat.

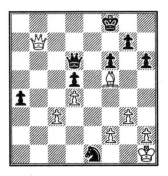

Carlsen – Ding Liren
Internet 2020
Black to move

12

Black has just captured on e1. There is no immediate threat to his knight. But having an unprotected piece on a distant square triggered his sense of danger.

He could protect the knight with 31...♕e7. The added benefit is that 32 ♕xe7+? would hand Black a winning endgame.

But 32 ♕a6! would win either the a-pawn or d-pawn. On top of that, Black's knight would remain endangered, by 32...♘f3 33 ♗e6! and ♗xd5.

This explains **31...♘f3**. Black wanted to safeguard the knight well before it is threatened.

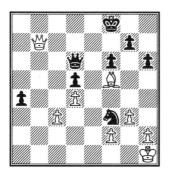

White to move

But he missed White's near-term threat, a mate after **32 ♗g6!** and ♕f7.

For example, 32...♕e6 33 ♕b4+ and mates. Or 32...♔g8 33 ♕f7+ ♔h8 35 ♕e8+.

Black's best defense was 31...♕e7 after all. Then he could continue 32 ♕a6! ♔f7! and ...g6, e.g. 33 ♕b5 g6 34 ♕xd5+ ♔g7 (35 ♗e6 a3!).

Dealing with the long-term threat, 31...♘f3??, was fatal.

Alarm Shut-Off

Even if you have a good sense of danger you can inadvertently turn this alarm system off. This often happens when you cannot imagine how your unprotected pieces can be attacked.

13

Carlsen – Giri
Internet 2020
White to move

White has a fairly wide choice of what we call candidate moves. Candidates are the most appealing moves you can consider playing.

For example, White might pick 25 ♘e3, which improves the placement of his knight. Another candidate is the safety-minded 25 ♗b1, which denies Black his only forcing move, …♘xd3+.

But why does White need safety? All of his pieces are protected except his rooks. And they can't be attacked, can they?

This led the world champion to play **25 f3**. It gave him options such as launching a kingside attack with ♖f2, fxg4 and ♗e2.

But he didn't look for a threat. He was lost after **25…♘xd3+ 26 ♕xd3 ♕c1+** and **27…♕xb2**.

False Security

Carlsen's sense of security misled him because Black's pieces seemed too far way. Your feeling of danger can be blunted in another way – when you believe you are making progress. Here is a typical scenario:

You make a threat. Your opponent parries it, by dodging, protecting or retreating. Then you make another threat. You begin to feel you command an initiative. You are the only one capable of forcing moves.

Nakamura – Carlsen
Internet 2020
White to move

Hikaru Nakamaura had been forcing matters for the previous eight moves.

Feeling optimistic, he was unwilling to accept a drawish trade of rooks, 26 ♖xd8+ ♖xd8 27 ♖xd8+ ♕xd8.

Instead, he sought additional forcing moves, **26 ♖d7** and then **26...♖xd7 27 ♖xd7**.

Good things can happen after 27...♕e8 28 a4 and better ones after 27...♖h1+ 28 ♔c2. This is the kind of thing that happens when your initiative continues.

Carlsen replied **27...♕b4!**.

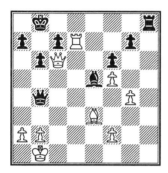

White to move

Black threatened mate on b2 but also ...♕xg4. This forced **28 ♗d4!**.

Nakamura still had reason to feel hopeful about his winning chances because there were ways he could win immediately (28...♗xd4?? 29 ♕xc7+ and mates).

On the other hand, he would have no more than a draw after 28...♕e1+ 29 ♔c2 ♕e2+.

When Carlsen replied **28...♗d6**, it should have set off an alarm. Why would he retreat when he could make unlimited queen checks?

White to move

15

Nakamura began to appreciate why. If he moves his attacked bishop, Carlsen would play ...♕xg4.

In addition, Nakamura could not play 29 ♕c3 because of 29...♖h1+! 30 ♔c2 ♕a4+ and...♕xd7.

But **29 ♕e4** looked safe.

The truth was revealed by **29...♕a4!**. The threats of 30...♕d1 mate and 30...♕xd7 prompted resignation.

Why did White collapse so quickly? The illusion of making progress earlier in the game concealed the dangers that led to 26 ♖d7? and 29 ♕e4??.

Threat Blindness

This illustrates one of the many ironies of chess. The player who can quickly see how to make threats can become myopic when his opponent surprises him with a threat.

Wade – Gligorić
Saltsjöbaden 1952
White to move

White should be feeling very good about his position. He has an extra pawn and a potential mating attack with 36 ♖d2!, threatening 37 ♖d7!.

He preferred **36 ♖f2**. Then he could activate his knight. For example, 36...♗g7 37 ♘f5! gets him close to a win.

He didn't have to worry about 36...♗xh4 because 37 gxh4 would open the g-file for a strong queen or rook check.

Black played the somewhat surprising **36...♕g5**.

16

White to move

White's advantage looks decisive. He naturally searched for a forcing move.

Instead of the move he intended, 37 ♘f5!, he attacked the queen with **37 ♖f5**.

It made tactical sense: 37...♕xg3 38 ♖xf6. But it was a false thread because after **37...♕g7** his rook occupied the best square for his knight.

Nevertheless, he was still winning. His position has been so good that he could retrace his steps with 38 ♖f2! and ♘f5!.

Computers have no problem recommending this. Humans want to make progress. White chose **38 ♘f3** with the idea of ♘d2-c4.

Black to move

White didn't realize it, but his winning advantage had vanished after **38...♖c6!**.

By protecting the bishop, Black threatened 39...♕xg3!. He also set a trap, 39 ♘xe5? ♖c5! and wins.

When your opponent can suddenly make a threat or set a trap, it should warn you that his tactical energy is growing. Here White should have looked for a second threat.

He would have spotted the potential mating attack begun by 39...♕d7! and ...♕d1.

White could defend with 39 ♘d2 or 39 ♘e1 and 40 ♘d3. Chances would be roughly even after 39...♕xg3.

But his sense of danger was failing when he stopped the first threat, ...♕xg3, with **39 g4**.

He needed to refocus after **39...♕d7!**.

White to move

White was not prepared to think of the abject defensive steps 40 ♖h5! and 41 ♖h2.

He tried one more forcing move, **40 g5**. His idea was 40...hxg5 41 ♖xf6! ♖xf6 42 ♘xg5, when anything can happen.

But he overlooked, **40...♕d1!**. He resigned after **41 ♘d4 ♕c1+** in view of 42 ♔a2 ♕d2+ 43 ♔a3 ♗e7+.

Each of White's earlier moves looked positive, even 38 ♘f3??. This was the problem.

What to Remember

"What does he threaten?" is the first checklist question because threats account for the greatest number of the critical moments of a chess game.

"What is his threat?" is the wrong question because there may be more than one. And you can't always count on a sense of security because it fails when you feel your opponent's pieces are too far away or when you are forcing matters and making progress.

When you spot a threat, a good procedure is: First, see if you have a defense. If the answer is yes, look for a second threat. If there is none, you can go back to the first threat and see if there are better ways of meeting it.

Quiz

Let's elaborate on the themes of this question with quiz positions. The answers can be found beginning on page 234.

1.

Firouzja – Giri
Internet 2020
Black to move

Black's **58...♖f2** threatened ...♖xf3+. What was wrong with this?

2.

Vaganian – Adorján
Thessaloniki 1984
White to move

Black's queen is trapped but he is not ready to resign. What should White do?

3.

Santos Latasa – Shirov
Leon 2020
Black to move

Black's earlier advantage was gone. What was wrong with **45...♗e6** ?

4.

Warmerdam – Eljanov
Wijk aan Zee 2020
Black to move

What did **18...♖c4** threaten?

5.

Adams – Harikrishna
Biel 2020
White to move

White averted ...♛xd3 with **40 d4**. Was this wrong?

6.

Saduakassova – Smirnov
Wijk aan Zee 2020
White to move

What should White do?

Chapter Two:
What Are The Tactical Ideas?

If the answer to "What does he threaten?" is "Nothing," this is good news. But it usually means you will have a harder time choosing your next move.

It will be harder because you are freed to consider more candidate moves.

The task of evaluating them begins with tactics. Whether you are a Petrosian fan or a would-be Tal, you are likely to look first at any move that threatens mate or gives check.

Carlsen – Xiong
Internet 2020
Black to move

Magnus Carlsen's last move, 34 g4, threatened the Black rook. Rather than move it to g5 or take on e5, Black chose **34...♖f3**.

A natural reply is 35 ♔g2 – natural because it threatens the rook again. But Carlsen instantly replied **35 g5!**.

He knew the game was over because of checkmate (36 ♖h4 or 36 ♖cc8 and 37 ♖h8).

If the enemy king is not a factor, the best tactic is one that attacks two undefended pieces at once. The more pieces your opponent leaves unguarded, the more likely that you have a chance for a winning double attack.

There are uncounted examples of this at the lowest levels of competitive chess. Here is one at the highest.

Caruana – Nakamura
Internet 2020
White to move

In a lost endgame, White played **41 ♘xd6?**.

When an experienced player examines a position, he looks for unprotected pieces. Good tacticians have trained themselves to do this subconsciously.

The better the tactician, the quicker he will find a double attack.

It only took Black seconds to prompt resignation with **41...♖f6!**.

Quick Sight

It took him only seconds because of his "quick sight." This is a rapid awareness of where the unprotected pieces are and how they can be attacked.

Hellers – Bareev
Gausdal 1986

1 e4 e6 2 d4 d5 3 ♘c3 ♘f6 4 ♗g5 ♗e7 5 e5 ♘fd7 6 h4 h6 7 ♗e3 c5 8 ♕g4 g6 9 ♘f3 ♘c6 10 dxc5 ♘xc5 11 0-0-0 a6 12 ♗xc5 ♗xc5 13 ♘e4 ♗e7 14 ♕f4 b5 15 ♘d6+ ♗xd6 16 exd6 ♖a7

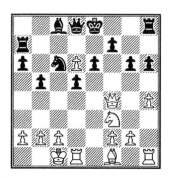

White to move

Black anticipated ♘e5/♕xf7 mate with his last move. But it served as an unintended hint for **17 ♘d4!**.

White threatens Black's unprotected knight. The second and more important point of 17 ♘d4 is that the unprotected Black rooks would be forked after 17...♘xd4 18 ♕xd4. Or after 17...♗d7 18 ♘xc6 ♗xc6 19 ♕d4.

Black tried the desperate **17...♔d7** but resigned after **18 ♗xb5! axb5 19 ♕xf7+** in view of 19...♔xd6 20 ♘xb5+ and ♘xa7.

Quick sight is a way of speed-reading the position. You can train yourself to do it by examining each new position you see and finding the pieces that are unprotected. Then see if those pieces can be attacked. Once you feel comfortable doing that you may find you do it subconsciously.

Pattern Recognition

If there are few or no unprotected enemy pieces, you have to search for a tactical shot. The search is easier if the position contains a tactical pattern.

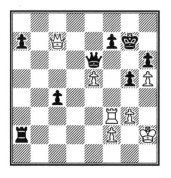

Aronian – Nepomniachtchi
Internet 2020
Black to move

White has prepared 40 ♖f6. Black quickly played the winning **39...♕d5!**.

The rook on f3 is attacked and cannot be defended (40 ♔g2 g4). Once it moves, 40...♖a1! sets up mate on h1.

One of the myths of chess is that it takes imagination to find tactics. Not true.

Recognizing tactical patterns is one of the very few skills that can come from rote learning – that is, repetition and memorization.

Memorization is possible because only a few pieces and pawns make up a pattern. In the last example, the pattern consisted of the Black queen at d5 and rook a1, the White king at h2 and the pawns at f2 and g3. Once Black recognized that there was a mate on h1 he just had to make sure the other White pieces did not prevent the mate.

In the pre-Internet days, diligent players would collect quiz-like positions to drill themselves over and over, to see what patterns they remembered. The father of the Polgar sisters regularly challenged his daughters with some 200,000 diagrams, many of them cut out of magazines he had collected.

Today you don't need a pair of scissors for this kind of training. There are quiz positions on various Web sites and in many books to train you. It can be a form of daily exercise. Even when Vishy Anand was world champion he tested himself on half a dozen quiz diagrams each day.

Combination Patterns

Tactics are the building blocks of combinations. It should not be a surprise, therefore, that most combinations are based on patterns.

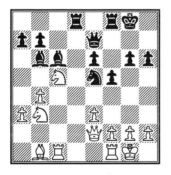

Nguyen – Samadashvili
St. Louis 2020
Black to move

Black can reason her way to finding the best move. But recognizing a basic pattern is faster: **1...♘f3+!** wins.

We call it "recognizing" – in the original sense of "to recognize," to recall to mind. Once Black recalled the pattern, the hardest part was over.

As combinations go, the main line was relatively simple to work out, **2 gxf3 ♕g5+ 3 ♔h1 ♕h5** and ...♗xf3+ (4.e4 ♗c7).

The only side line to calculate is 2 ♔h1, which allows 2...♕d6! 3 gxf3 ♗c7! and mates.

Students may feel overwhelmed by the number of patterns that can be committed to memory. But you don't need to know them all. A pioneering program, Hitech, played at 2100 strength. Then it was "taught" 40 basic tactical patterns and gained 200 points to become a strong master.

What students should be surprised by is how *few* original combinations there are. The combinations that grandmasters play today – and have played for decades – are usually variations on familiar themes. The masters' greatest task is recognizing a pattern of four or five pieces that is hidden amid many extraneous pieces and pawns.

Uhlmann – Smyslov
Moscow 1956
Black to move

No pattern is evident. But imagine that the d4-knight was gone and the caption read, "Black to move and win."

Then most experienced players would see 15...♝xf2+!.

The main line is one of the oldest tactical patterns, using just queen and knight checks – 16 ♔xf2 ♞g4+ 17 ♔g1 ♛e3+ 18 ♔h1 ♞f2+.

There is even a mating pattern at the end: 19 ♔g1 ♞h3+! is better than 19...♞xd1+ because of the smothered mate 20 ♔h1 ♛g1+! 21 ♖xg1 ♞f2.

Once Black recognized the pattern of queen and knight checks, he realized he needed to get rid of the knight in the diagram.

Armed with those clues he found **15...♞c2!** based on 16 ♛xc2 ♝xf2+ 17 ♔xf2 ♞g4+. Or 17 ♔h1 ♝xe1 18 ♖xe1 d4!.

Of course, the more patterns you know, the greater your tactical armory. The Deep Blue program that defeated Garry Kasparov in 1997 "knew" several times the patterns that Hitech did two decades before. But to compete with masters you need to know only a fraction of that.

Opened Line

If there is no detectable pattern, a tactical opportunity will leave clues in the position for you to find. One is the opening of a diagonal, rank or file. When a line is cleared of obstacles, a good tactician's eyes light up.

Ivanchuk – Seirawan
Groningen 1997
White to move

Black has only one active piece, his rook. But it can become dangerous after 29 ♕b1 ♕a7! and ...♖a1/...♘e5.

White took what seemed like a natural precaution. He safeguarded his first rank with **29 ♗f1**.

What he overlooked was this exposed his second rank after **29...d5!**.

The threat of 30...♕xh2 mate conferred on Black a big advantage, e.g. 30 ♗f2? ♕f4, and wins (31 ♕e1 ♘e5 and ...♘f3+).

Note how innocuous 29 ♗f1?? looked before 29...d5. This is often the case with moves that fatally open a toxic line. Here is how two of the world's best players overlooked this factor.

Nakamura – Carlsen
Internet 2020
White to move

Nakamura's **12 f4** was a typical Sicilian Defense idea. He prepared 13 e5, so that 13...dxe5 would allow 14 ♗xh7+ and 15 ♖xd8.

Carlsen answered **12...e5**, a typical defense in similar positions.

Only after the game did they realize they had both blundered. Black could have won material with 12...♗xe3+! 13 ♕xe3 ♘g4!.

White's queen must abandon the opened a7-g1 diagonal and allow 14...♕a7+ and 15...♘e3!.

Double Edged

Only Black could benefit from the opened diagonal in the last example. But when lines are cleared they often provide opportunities for both players.

Groszpeter – Tal
Sochi 1984
Black to move

Mikhail Tal saw how 31...♗xa3 could set up an elementary skewer, 32 ♖xd4? ♗c5.

But White would have some compensation for his lost pawn after 32 ♖g2 and ♗f2. So, Tal turned to **31...f5** for two tactical reasons.

First, he threatened 32...f4 33 ♗h4 ♗xa3.

Second, he also hoped to blow open the diagonal leading to White's king with 32... fxe4 33 fxe4 ♖xe4!.

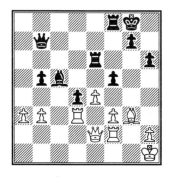

White to move

White replied **32 ♖g2**. It provided a retreat for his bishop after 32...f4.

And it avoided immediate disaster on the long diagonal after **32... fxe4 33 fxe4 ♖xe4**.

But he was lost after 34 ♕d1 ♕e7 because of the newly opened e-file.

For example, 35 a4 ♗d6! (36 ♗xd6? ♖e1+ or 36 ♖g1 ♕b7 37 ♖g2 ♖fe8).

You can claim Tal was lucky. He took an unnecessary risk with 31...f5?!. It opened *another* diagonal, the one leading to his king.

White could have exploited it with 32 b4! followed by ♕a2!.

Black to move (after 32 b4!)

Now 32...fxe4? fails to 33 bxc5 exd3? 34 ♕xe6+.

So, 32... ♗b6 33 ♕a2! is critical.

The pin on the a2-g8 diagonal would shrink Tal's winning chances (33...♕d7 34 exf5 ♖xf5 35 ♖e2).

29

But this is why a well-trained tactician wins – and is called lucky. He takes better advantage than his opponent of an opened position that could have gone either way.

Queen Clue

Another tactical tipoff occurs when a player advances his queen to a potentially perilous square.

Nunn – Miles
London 1982
Black to move

White's queen is lined up on the same diagonal as the g7-bishop.

But the immediate attacks on it, 17...♘e4 or 17...♘d7, lose to 19 ♕xg7. And 17...♘h5? 18 ♕e3 d4 19 ♖xd4 is poor.

However, the idea of attacking the queen is so appealing that Black searched for a way to enhance it. He found that the unlikely **17...♖g8!** was strong.

White had to safeguard his queen, with **18 ♕a4**.

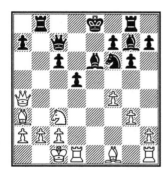

Black to move

But after **18...♕b6** he threatened powerful knight moves, ...♘g4-f2, ...♘d7-c5 or 19...♘e4 20 ♘xe4 ♗xb2+.

Play went **19 ♗g2 ♘d7! 20 ♖d3 ♗f5!** and White was lost after **21 ♖e1+ ♔d8 22 ♖f3? ♖e8! 23 ♖xe8+ ♔xe8** in view of ...♘c5 or ...♕g1+.

A beginner is often bewildered by the many do's and don'ts of chess instruction. This example illustrated one of the most important don'ts: Do not give up quickly on an appealing idea, tactical or positional. Try to see if it can be improved and turned into a strong move.

Tradeoff

If a queen can get into trouble so quickly, why do good players advance it early in a game? The answer is a queen is by far the best piece for making double attacks.

There is a fundamental tradeoff for an aggressive piece. The farther it advances, the more it may threaten – and be threatened.

Golubev – Lupulescu, Bucharest 2002

1 e4 c5 2 ♘f3 d6 3 d4 cxd4 4 ♘xd4 ♘f6 5 ♘c3 ♘c6 6 ♗c4 ♕b6 7 ♘xc6 bxc6 8 0-0 g6 9 ♕e1 ♘g4 10 h3 ♘e5

Now 11 ♗b3 ♗a6! 12 ♗e3 ♕c7 13 ♘e2 ♗g7 is fine for Black. So, **11 ♘a4! ♕d4 12 ♗b3 ♗a6** was played.

White to move

White appears to be in trouble because of 13...♗xf1.

He can complicate matters with 13 ♗e3 ♕xe4 14 f3! and 14...♕f5 15 f4!. Then 15...♗xf1 16 fxe5 ♗xg2! is double-edged.

White can conclude that 13 ♗e3 is a good way out of a difficult position. But is it the best way of exploiting Black's queen?

White found **13 ♗d2!**, threatening to win it with 14 ♗c3.

Black created an escape route with **13...f5.**

White to move

Again White has a good answer, 14 ♗c3 ♛xe4 15 f4!. He would emerge with a major material edge after 15...♗xf1 16 ♛xf1 and fxe5.

But even better was **14 ♗e3! ♛xe4 15 f3!**. The f5-square was unavailable to the queen now and Black lost after **15...♘xf3+ 16 ♖xf3**.

Underprotected

If a pawn or piece is defended as many times as it is attacked, it seems safe. But it can turn out to be *underprotected.*

This happens when one more attacker is easily added and there is no additional defender.

Giri – Vachier-Lagrave
Internet 2020
Black to move

The only White piece that seems in danger is his knight. But it is only potential danger. If Black threatens it with 25...♛g4, White can defend with 26 ♘c3 or 26 b3.

But Black needs to make sure, by calculating further. When he does, he sees nothing wrong with 26 ♘c3.

However, he would notice that 26 b3?? has a big tactical flaw – 26...♖d1!.

He wins after 27 ♖f2 ♕e4+ and then 28 ♖f3 ♕xf3+ or 28 ♔g1 ♖xf1+ 29 ♕xf1 ♗d4.

But so what? Why does this matter if there is nothing wrong with 26 ♘c3 ?

It matters because it whispered a hint to Black: The White piece most vulnerable is not the knight but the one on f1.

He played **25...♖d1!**

White to move

The f1-rook is protected, but Black can add another attacking piece. One way is 26...♕f3!. Another is 26...♖fd8! followed by 27...♖xf1+ and 28...♖d1.

White's predicament is that he can't add another defender of his rook. He would lose after 26 ♔g1 ♗d4+ and 26 ♖f2 ♗xg3 27 ♖xd1 ♗xf2 28 ♕d3 ♖e8.

The prettiest loss is 26 ♖gg1 ♗d4! with a mating threat of 27...♕f3+!.

Thanks to 25...♖d1!, the f1-rook is shown to be underprotected. White can prolong the game with 26 g4. But 26...♖xf1+ 27 ♕xf1 ♕g5 would be hard to survive.

Instead, the game went **26 ♕c4?? ♕f3!**.

White resigned in view of 27 ♖g1 ♖fd8 followed by 28...♖8d2 or 28...♖xg1+ and 28...♖d1+.

Overworked

Similar to an underprotected piece is its brother, an overworked piece. It serves guard duty. But like many sentries it has too much to guard at one time.

Carlsen – Ding Liren
Internet 2020
White to move

Quick sight tells White there is one unprotected piece, the g8-rook. He played **22 ♕h7!**.

The only way to save the rook is to move the e8-bishop. This is the piece that Black has protected the most. But it costs him the game because it is overworked.

For example, 22...♗h5 loses the queen to 23 ♘d7+.

Trickier is 22...♗c6. But both 23 bxc6 fxe5 24 ♖ab1 and 23 ♗xa5 ♕xa5 24 ♘c4 ♕xc3 25 ♖fc1 would win.

Purdy's Protection Principle

It is good to have your pieces and pawns protected before they are attacked. This is obvious. The great teacher C. J. S. Purdy added:

"But it is not so good to protect them when actually attacked."

How can this be true? The answer is that after a player manages to defend an attacked piece, it is his opponent's turn. If he can distract the defender, the chain of protection collapses.

J. Polgar – Timman
Wijk aan Zee 2003
White to move

Black's knight and rook are unprotected. A good tactician quickly spots the double attack 27 ♕d6.

But 27 ♕d6 leaves White's bishop unprotected. After 27 ♕d6? ♖f8 28 ♕xc5 Black can reply 28...♕xe2 and be quite safe.

The idea of exploiting the undefended knight is too good to abandon quickly. Before looking elsewhere White found **27 ♖c1!**.

This also threatens the knight but it has tactical benefits based on pins – 27...♖c8 28 b4! and 27...♕c6 28 b4!.

Black needed to protect the knight but also wanted to rule out ♕d6. He chose **27...♕e5**.

White to move

But the chain of protection was broken by **28 f4!**.

Black would lose soon after 28...♕c7 29 b4 or slowly after 28...♘e4 29 fxe5! ♘xd2 30 ♔f2.

He tried **28...♕f5**. This left his other pieces unprotected and exploited by **29 ♕d6!**.

35

Black allowed a pin, **29...♖c8 30 b4**, and then resigned after **30...♕e4 31 ♕d2**.

Each of his final moves met the immediate danger. But then it was his opponent's turn to move.

An overworked piece can also be exploited by exchanging it.

Tiviakov – Kupreichik
Moscow 1989
White to move

This could appear in a quiz with the caption "White to move and win." But suppose the caption read "Which three Black pieces are most vulnerable?" This would be a harder task.

The win begins with **11 ♗f3**.

Black would lose one of the rooks after 11...♕a5 12 ♘xc6 bxc6 13 ♗xc6+.

This led to **11...♕c4 12 ♘xc6 bxc6**

White to move

White attacks one rook with **13 ♕d4!** and eliminates the overworked defender of c6 after **13...♕xd4 14 ♗xd4**.

So the answer to the second quiz question is, "The queen and both rooks are vulnerable." Black could have resigned in light of 14...e5 15 ♗xc6+ or 15 ♗xe5 dxe5 16 ♗xc6+.

Anticipating Tactics

The examples in this book come mainly from grandmaster games. Why do strong players fall victim to what seems like simple moves?

One explanation is they did not ask themselves the same questions that their opponent did, starting with "What are the tactical ideas?"

Ljubojević – Smyslov
Skopje 1972
Black to move

Black has active options, such as the forcing 18...♘e7. But he chose **18...♖fe8**.

It seems mysterious – until you ask "What are the tactical ideas?"

Black asked and had an answer. White did not and the game went **19 ♖ad1?? ♗f8!**.

Black played ...♖fe8 because he noticed a tactic, the pin of the queen with ...♗f8 and ...♗c5. White made this idea much stronger by leaving his a3-knight unprotected.

If he safeguards the knight and queen with 20 ♕a1, Black would win with 20...♕c5+ and 21...♕xa3.

Instead, White saved his piece with **20 b4 ♗xb4 21 ♕a1**. He lost the endgame after **21...♕c5+ 22 d4 ♕c3!**.

Another way to anticipate your opponent's best tactical idea is to think twice when you put a piece on an unprotected square.

This sounds too cautious. In most cases your unprotected piece will not be vulnerable. But in those other instances...

Carlsen – Xiong
Internet 2020
Black to move

White's best tactical chances rest on his a-pawn and in Black's chain of protected pieces. He can try to exploit both elements with 34 ♖c1 (34...♖c8? 35 ♖xc7 and queens). Black's main choice is between 33...♗d5 and 33...♗g4. Both have merits.

For example, 33...♗d5! attacks the queen but also protects his rook after 34 ♕b8+ ♘e8. Then he can consolidate (35 ♘f4 ♗b7 and ...♕c7). Note how well Black's pieces guard one another.

But Black thought **33...♗g4**, attacking the unprotected knight, was better.

He overlooked **34 ♕b8+!**. The unprotected bishop fell (**34...♕f8 35 ♘f6+**) and White won.

Thought Routes

"What are the tactical ideas?" is a shortcut to finding tactical tricks, and this is why it is on the checklist. But as we will see in pages to come, there is often more than one path to finding the same best move.

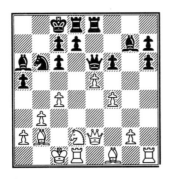

Nepomniachtchi – Giri
Internet 2020
White to move

White can detect a hidden tactic by wondering:

"Are any Black pieces unprotected? Yes, that bishop on a6. How can I get at it?"

Or, he may have thought:

"My e5-pawn is threatened. If I defend it with 17 ♘f3, I have problems after 17...dxe5 18 fxe5 d5. I need something sharper. What else is there?"

Still another way is:

"I'd like to play 17 exf6. But 17...♗xf6 seems pretty even. Is there a better way to use the exf6 idea?"

All three thought routes could lead him to **17 ♘e4!**.

It threatens a forking ♘c5 as well as a capture on f6. Black would be in bad shape after 17...♕f7 18 exf6 or 17...♗b7 18 ♘xf6.

He became desperate, sacrificed the bishop, **17...fxe5 18 ♘c5 ♕f5 19 ♘xa6**, and slowly lost.

Was ♘c5 the only tactical idea hidden in the diagram?

No, if White takes the first route ("Are there any unprotected Black pieces?") he might also have found 17 ♕f2!.

The point is that 17...fxe5? 18 c5! wins (18...♗xf1 19 cxb6!).

What to Remember

There are various way to find the tactical ideas in a position. The most common are recognizing a pattern, spotting unprotected pieces or a vulnerable queen, and appreciating what the opening of a line means for you and your opponent's pieces.

These are trainable skills. More difficult to master is realizing what overworked and unprotected pieces are. But there is no faster way to improve in chess than to improve your tactics.

Quiz

7.

Bologan – Smirnov
Moscow 2003
Black to move

Black handed his opponent a tactic with **35...♘c5**. Which?

8. Carlsen – Xiong, Internet 2020

1 c4 c5 2 ♘c3 g6 3 e3 ♘f6 4 d4 cxd4 5 exd4 d5 6 ♕b3 ♗g7 7 cxd5 0-0 8 ♗e2 ♘a6 9 ♗f3 b5 10 ♘ge2 ♖b8 11 ♗f4 ♖b6 12 ♘xb5

Black to move

Was White's capture risky?

9.

Grischuk – Aronian
Internet 2020
Black to move

The best winning try is **37...d4!**. What did Black intend after **38 exd4** ?

10.

Svidler – Grandelius
Internet 2020
Black to move

In check, Black didn't like 26...♕e8 27 ♕xe8+ and ♗xb7. What was wrong with **26....♘e8** ?

11.

Aronin – Geller
Moscow 1950
Black to move

How should Black continue?

12.

Boleslavsky – Goldberg
Moscow 1945
Black to move

Black saw the threat of 13 b4 and played **12...c5**. Did that save him?

13.

Taimanov – Antoshin
Moscow 1956
White to move

Black's last move, 29...♛e6, gave White an idea. Which?

14.

Karpov – Torre
Leningrad 1973
White to move

Black's queen is vulnerable. But 22 g4? ♛f7 23 ♘g5?? ♛xf2+ is not possible. What is?

15.

Korobov – Bu
Internet 2020
Black to move

One White piece is exploitable. Which?

16.

Karpov – Portisch
Tilburg 1988
Black to move

Black did not want to play the ♕+♗-vs.-♕+♘ endgame after 51...♖xb3. He chose **51...♖a1**.Why was that wrong?

17.

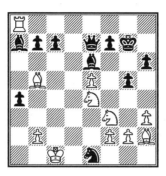

Grischuk – Giri
Internet 2020
White to move

In a chaotic position, is **26 ♘xe1** the best move?

18.

Karpov – Timman
Amsterdam 1991
White to move

Exploiting the eighth rank with 23 ♖c8+ ♖d8 24 ♗c7 loses to 24...♛e1+. What is better?

19.

Ljubojević – Ciocâltea
Vršac 1971
White to move

Black had played 13...♕e5 in hopes of forcing 14 ♕xe5. How should White respond?

20.

Miles – Gonzáles Mestres
Las Palmas 1980
White to move

Black's last move, 22...♖(e8)e7, created a tactical opportunity for White. Which?

21.

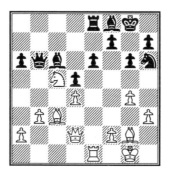

Timman – Khalifman
Amsterdam 1995
White to move

Black's minor pieces appear well protected. How can White change this?

22.

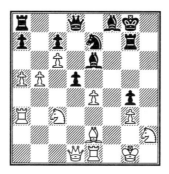

Giri – Korobov
Internet 2020
White to move

Black lost after **26 exd5 ♞xd5 27 ♗c4**. What did he miss?

23.

Lputian – Ivanchuk
Montecatini Terme 2000
Black to move

Black can try 24...♝c6 or 24...♝h3. Is there a better move?

24.

Shimanov – Kamsky
Tromsø 2013
White to move

Play went **20 ♖f2 ♞g3 21 ♞f3**. What did both players miss?

Chapter Three:
What Is Wrong With His Move?

The biggest natural advantage in chess is the right to make the next move of the game. David Bronstein said this.

We can add: The game's *last* move is nearly as important.

The move your opponent has just made provides you with the best clue to finding the best reply.

The reason is that every move changes the position, however slightly. The moving piece gains control of new squares. But it also gives up control of others.

Siegbert Tarrasch was exaggerating – just a bit – when he said every chess move weakens some part of the position, except for a move that delivers checkmate.

Dubov – Nakamura
Internet 2020
Black to move

Players with quick sight will immediately see White is threatening a ♗c7 fork.

If you take a longer look, you may realize 16 ♖c7 would also win. So would 16 f4 and 16 ♗h7+ (16...♔xh7 17 ♕xf7+). White's position is that good.

Black stopped the primary threat, ♗c7, as well as ♖c7 with **15...e5**.

White can begin extensive calculating to see if 16 f4 and 16 ♗h7+ still win. (They do.)

But masters typically find the best moves with less calculation than non-masters. They will spot the major drawback of 15...e5.

By closing one, diagonal, g3 to c7, it opened another diagonal, b3 to f7.

This made **16 ♗c4!** a killer. The threat was 17 ♕xf7+ and 18 ♕g8 mate.

The game could end with 16...♖d7 17 ♕g6+ ♗g7 18 ♘f5 or 17...♔h8 18 ♗xf7.

Instead, it went **16...♕c7 17 ♗xe5 resigns**.

Significantly

You don't need Tarrasch to tell you that the position changes when your opponent moves. What you want to know is whether it changes significantly.

You start by looking for reasons his move might help him, such as by protecting an undefended piece. The second step should be to look for reasons his move may hurt him.

Why would he make a move that hurts him? Because he is too focused on how it helps him.

Gelfand – Morozevich
Zürich 2016
Black to move

White has just moved his queen from b1. When Black looks for a threat, he sees 45 ♕e6 mate.

He could create a flight square for the king with, for example, 45...♗e7. But he noticed a second threat, 46 ♗f3 and ♕xc6.

He chose **45...♕d6**.

White saw how this helps Black: It averts ♕e6 mate and allows Black to push ...c5 in case of ♗f3.

But White looked beyond the benefits and tried to find how it hurts Black. He spotted **46 c5!**.

That clears c4 for a deadly bishop check. Black had nothing better than 46...♛e7 47 ♗c4+ ♚e8, and eventually lost after 48 ♛xc6+ and cxb6.

Impressionist

An opponent's move may suggest a specific reply, such as 46 c5! in that example. Or it can instill a general impression.

It may just be a vague impression, a feeling you can express more easily in words than in moves.

Smyslov – Dzindzichashvili
Moscow 1972
Black to move

If you were to describe this position, you might cite a lot of moves:

"White threatens ♘xb6. Black can defend it with 16...♛c7. Then White can expand on the queenside with 17 a3 and 18 b4. Or, perhaps he chould maneuver his pieces, such as ♘c2-e3."

But after **16...♘d7**, you might be struck by a thought: "There are no Black pieces around his king."

This is does not tell you what move to play. But it suggests what kind: It should be something forceful on the kingside, not a maneuver or a quiet move on the queenside.

Once you sense the drawback to 16...♘d7 you might ask a checklist question we will get to later, "What is his weakest point?"

The answer is g7, followed by e6. This helps you think of specific moves.

White to move

With 17 ♕g4, the queen is one knight move away from ♕xg7 mate.

Then you begin analyzing and find the mating idea is easily thwarted by 17...♘de5!.

So, you take another look at the position. But you can't get away from the feeling that Black's king is vulnerable.

You might turn to 17 ♗h3. It makes a different threat, 18 ♘xe6 fxe6 19 ♗xe6+ and ♗xd7.

But again calculation disappoints you: The threat of ♘xe6 is extinguished by 17...♘xd4 18 ♗xd4 ♕c7.

However, that general impression should prompt you to look still further. Then you may see a mixture of the two tactical ideas, **17 ♘xe6! fxe6 18 ♕g4!**.

Black to move

This threatens ♕xg7 mate as well as ♕xe6+. Both of the weak points you noticed after 16...♘d7 have become real targets.

White would have more than enough compensation for his sacrificed knight after 18...♘de5 19 ♕xe6+ ♘f7 20 ♘xb6, for example.

Or after 18...♔f7 19 ♕xg7+ ♔e8 20 ♕g8+.

Instead, the game went **18...♘f6 19 ♕xe6+ ♔h8 20 ♘xb6 ♖f8? 21 c5 ♖a7 22 cxd6 ♗d8 23 ♘a4 ♖e8 24 ♕f7 ♗a8 25 d7 ♖g8 26 ♕e6 ♕b5** and Black resigned.

New Info

When the opening of a game blends into the middlegame, the position on the board contains basic information that guides you further:

It tells you which king is more vulnerable, what the tactical ideas are and how the pawn structure looks. You store this and other information in your mind.

You do it subconsciously. You don't have to tell yourself, "Material is equal. I must remember this." Or "I might have a good sacrifice on f6 in the future. I don't want to forget this."

As play continues, you acquire fresh, new information. You have to determine if it supersedes what you've stored.

Najer – Timofeev
Krasnoyarsk 2003
Black to move

As he waits for Black to move, White might be thinking:

"I like my position. I'm ahead in development. His weakest point seems to be g7. I can target it with ♕g4. Also, his rooks aren't connected yet. So I might play ♖xd8+ followed by ♖d1 and win control of the d-file."

When Black plays **19...0-0** the position has changed. His rooks are now connected and g7 is protected. None of White's stored information seemed useful.

But there is new information. The most important is revealed by asking, "What is wrong with his move?"

By castling, Black made h7 more vulnerable than g7. The most important line is not the d-file but the c2-h7 diagonal. Therefore **20 ♗c2!**.

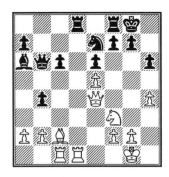

Black to move

Black cannot block the diagonal with 20...♘f5? because of 21 g4!.

Better, but still bad. is 20...f5 21 exf6 ♖xf6 in view of 22 ♕h7+ ♔f7 23 ♘e5+.

When Black chose **20...g6**, White needed a new idea. Again he should ask, "What is wrong with his move?"

One answer is that the h6-pawn has become weaker. But 21 ♕f4 is ineffective after 21...♖xd1+ 22 ♖xd1 ♗e2!.

The other new information provided by 20...g6 is that by shielding h7, Black exposed the g6-square. This prompted **21 h5!**.

Black to move

White threatened to win with 22 hxg6 followed by 22...♘xg6 23 ♘h4! or 22...fxg6 23 ♕g4.

There was no good defense, and after **21...♘f5** he might have won fastest with 22 hxg6 fxg6 23 ♖d6!.

If you have been a spectator at a simultaneous exhibition, you've witnessed how a master uses stored and new information. When he turns to the next board he can make his move quickly because he is relying on what he remembered.

54

But you probably witnessed something else. Before he started thinking at the new board, he wanted to know what his opponent's last move was. It is new information, the best clue to how he should reply.

Threat Backfire

Most of all, the simul-giver wants to know if his opponent has made a threat. Then the master can decide whether to parry the threat or ignore it – or look for its drawback.

Serper – Shirov
Moscow 1991
Black to move

White is looking for a knockout blow, such as 27 ♘e5 followed by 28 ♘g4 or 28 ♖xf6/29 ♕h5.

He might expect a defensive try such as 26...♕c8 and ...♕c1+.

Instead, Black tried to throw him off balance with **26...♘h5**.

What is the proper response to a surprise like this? You can start by asking yourself the first checklist question: What does he threaten?

Here the answer is 27...♘xf4. White can respond by analyzing continuations such as 27 ♖d4 ♗xf3.

But he can also look for a reason that 26...♘h5 is bad. He would see, for instance, that the h7-pawn is underprotected. This suggests 27 ♕c2.

If he calculates this move, he can find a win after 27...♘xf4? 28 ♗xh7+ ♔h8 29 ♘e5. But he'll find a messy position after 27...♗f6.

White to move

Is there a simpler try to punish 26...♘h5?

One thing to notice is that it opens part of the f-file. That feature suggests a tactical idea, ♖f8+.

White can calculate good results after 27 ♖f8+ ♖xf8 28 ♕xe6+. This looks at least as good as the 27 ♕c2 option.

But before he tries to choose between them he looks for something even simpler – **27 ♕xe6+!**.

Black resigned because of 27...♖xe6 28 ♖f8 mate.

This is how a threat can backfire. If your opponent surprises you with a threatening move, it may coax you to consider a response you would not normally consider.

Artemiev– Nepomniachtchi
Internet 2020
White to move

White needs to safeguard his king before 20...♖ad8 and 21...♕d1+! mates him.

He can do this with 20 ♔g1 and 20 ♗d5. More daring is 20 g4. It looks risky but by threatening the f5-bishop it also frees a square for 21 ♔g2!.

White preferred **20 ♘g3** with the idea of 21 ♘xf5. He would be safe after 20...♗d3+ 21 ♔g1.

But 20 ♘g3 prompted Black to think about other moves for his bishop.

He found **20...♗b1!**.

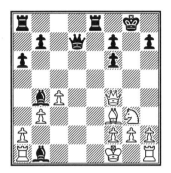

White to move

Mate is threatened with 21...♖e1. And 21 ♖xb1 would lose to 21...♕d3+ and ...♕xb1+.

White had nothing better than 21 ♕c1 ♖e1+ 22 ♕xe1 ♗xe1. Instead, he went down faster following **21 ♔g1 ♖e1+ 22 ♘f1 ♕d3**.

Black won because 20 ♘g3?? unintentionally prompted him to notice the kind of move, 20...♗b1!, that might be out of his normal field of vision.

"Impossible" Moves

This illustrates yet another irony of chess: When you make a threat, you hope to severely limit your opponent's options. But you can dramatically widen them. You may be forcing an opponent to consider moves that seem impossible.

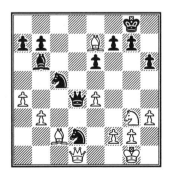

Butnorius – Cramling
Gibraltar 2007
White to move

Black's last move, ...♕d4, set the stage for a knight move followed by ...♕xf2+. Therefore, White played **31 ♘e2**.

Black has 40 legal replies. But because her queen was attacked she was limited to queen moves.

If it retreats to e5, she loses the d2-knight. If it goes to d7, then 32 a5! costs a piece (32...♕xe7 33 axb6).

The process of elimination appeared to leave only 30...♕b4, when chances would be equal.

But knowing that her queen had to move prompted her to look at all of its options. That included **32...♕xf2+!**.

It is based on 33 ♔xf2?? ♘cxe4+ 34 ♔e1 ♗f2 mate. White had to play **33 ♔h1** and lost after **33...♘cxe4**.

An "impossible" move may be justified by relatively short calculation. In this case, 33 ♔xf2 would allow mate in two moves. But the impossible may also be incalculable.

When this happens, you have to trust your intuition.

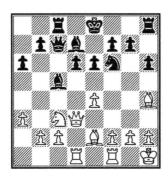

Geller – Vasiukov
Riga 1975
Black to move

White's last move, 14 ♔h1, seems out of character in a position that should be increasingly tactical. But Black understood what White wanted:

White prepared 15 f4 and with it a powerful threat of 16 e5! (16...dxe5 17 fxe5 ♕xe5? 18 ♗xf6 and ♕xd7+).

Black analyzed his options. He rejected, for example, 14...♗xa3 15 ♗xf6.

He decided to blockade the position. This meant taking a positional gamble, with **14...g5 15 ♗g3 e5**.

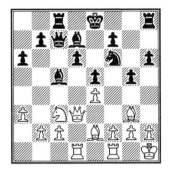

White to move

White can ask himself checklist questions that we will get to later in this book. For example, "Will my position get better with routine moves?" (Answer: No.)

Better questions are "What is his weakest point?" and "What is the principled move?" Both answers would lead him to the move he played.

He can also find it by asking what the positional drawback of 15...e5 is. The answer is that it surrenders pawn control of d5. If White can play ♘d5 without fear of ...♘xd5 in reply, he would have a huge strategic edge.

White chose **16 f4!**. He could exploit the d5-square after 16...gxf4? 17 ♗h4! (17...♘h7 18 ♘d5) with more than enough compensation for a pawn.

Play continued **16...exf4 17 ♗xf4! gxf4 18 ♖xf4**.

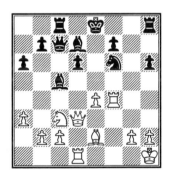

Black to move

Yefim Geller confessed in his notes that he could calculate 18...♕d8 19 ♖df1 and 18...♔e7 19 ♖xf6! but not the full ramifications of his piece sacrifice. He trusted his intuition about the weakness of f7.

After **18...♘h7** he got the better of **19 ♘d5 ♕d8 20 b4 ♗a7 21 e5** and eventually won.

His calculation failed him – 19 ♕g3 would have won much faster, as much later analysis showed. But his intuition did not. He was right about 16 f4!.

One After Another

Beginners are surprised by how a master manages to play one threatening move after another until he wins.

This is not magic. When you force your opponent to keep responding to threats, he may not have time to keep his pieces coordinated. You can stretch his pieces to the breaking point.

Carlsen – Caruana
Internet 2020
White to move

Magnus Carlsen has solid moves he could play without looking more than one move ahead. For example, 33 ♖a1 and 33 ♗d3 need little calculation.

But he chose **33 ♘e5** because it threatened 34 ♘xd7 followed by 35 ♕xb6.

His calculation was still relatively easy: 33...♖b5?? 34 ♕d8+ and 33...♘xe5? 34 ♕xb6 would lose.

As expected, Black answered **33...♖b8**.

What followed was a repeat of this process. Carlsen kept making threats that were based on Black's previous move. Black had to keep responding to the threats.

White to move

With **34 ♕a7!** Carlsen threatened the overworked d7-knight.

Then 34...♖d8 35 ♖b1 would threaten ♖b7.

He would win after 35...♘c8 36 ♕a8 ♘xe5? 37 dxe5 ♕xe5 38 ♖b8, for example. He would be closing in on a win after 36...♖f8 37 f4.

That led to **34...♘xe5 35 dxe5**.

Black realized the problem that 35...♕b4 36 ♕d7! would create. He retreated **35...♕d8**.

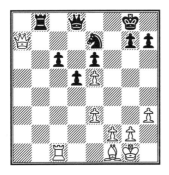

White to move

Carlsen expected this and had prepared a way to exploit it. He instantly played **36 ♗e2!**. Black's last move made the e6-pawn vulnerable.

Carlsen was setting the stage for 37 ♗g4!, followed by ♗xe6(+). Or 37...♘f5 38 ♗xf5 and ♖xc6.

Black did not trust flimsy defenses based on ...♔f7. He tried **36...♔h8**, so ♗xe6 would not be check.

Next came **37 ♗g4 ♘g6**.

This was a good practical stab at defense. Black would rebound after 38 ♗xe6? ♘xe5 or 38 ♖xc6?? ♖b1+ 39 ♔h2 ♘xe5.

White to move

Carlsen had temporarily run out of forcing moves. But as we'll see with a later checklist question, a good move can also be judged by what it stops, rather than what it threatens.

With **38 f4!** he stopped ...♘xe5. This made captures on c6 and e6 tactically possible and virtually decisive.

Black's pieces had been stretched as far as they could go (38...♕e8 39 ♗xe6! ♕xe6?? 40 ♕xb8+).

He was gradually ground down after **38...♖a8 39 ♕c5 ♕e8 40 ♕xc6**.

Petite Combinaison

Carlsen's moves from 33 ♘e5 on constituted an initiative. An initiative is usually defined as the ability to force matters by making threats.

Left out of the dictionary definition – but often present in the flesh – is the role of the last move.

A century earlier, José Capablanca often won with a Carlsen-like initiative. He gave it the misleading title of *petite combinaison*, a little combination. Here is an example.

Capablanca – Von Balla, Budapest 1928

1 d4 ♘f6 2 c4 e6 3 ♘c3 ♗b4 4 ♕c2 c5 5 dxc5 ♘c6 6 a3 ♗xc5 7 b4 ♗e7 8 ♘f3 ♕c7 9 g3 b6 10 ♗g2 ♗b7 11 ♗f4 d6

White to move

Black's last move doesn't look like an error but it created a target at d6 that proved to be fatal.

One way to exploit it was 12 c5. But this runs out of gas after 12...bxc5 13 bxc5 0-0! in view of 14 ♘b5? ♕a5+.

The right way is **12 ♘b5!**. Its power lies partly in 12...♕d7 13 ♖d1 d5 14 ♘c7+ and 13...e5 14 ♗xe5!.

The other part became apparent after **12...♕b8**.

Then 13 ♖d1 can be solidly met by 13...♘e5!. But stronger is **13 c5!**.

Black to move

Clearly, 13...♘e5? now fails to 14 cxd6, winning at least a piece.

Black had to settle for **13...e5**.

How hard was it for White to find his last two moves? Not very. He only needed to evaluate the few forcing moves available.

His next move was somewhat obvious, **14 cxd6**.

Black would be lost after 14...exf4 15 ♘c7+ (15...♔f8 16 dxe7+).

He was forced into **14...♗xd6**.

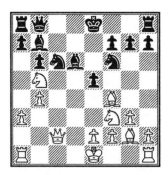

White to move

For the first time since 12 ♘b5, White had to put on his calculating cap. He needed to choose among three attractive alternatives.

The positional option, 15 ♗g5, would threaten to damage Black's pawn structure with 16 ♗xf6. White would have a nice middlegame ahead after 15...♗e7 16 ♘h4 prepared ♘f5!.

More forcing is the second option, 15 ♘xd6+ ♕xd6.

Then 16 ♘xe5 appears strong – until you see 16...♘d4!.

White can try to fine-tune this idea with 16 ♖d1. Then 16...♕b8 17 ♘xe5! works. But 16...♕e7! would hold his edge to a minimum.

Capablanca chose the powerful third option, **15 ♖d1!**.

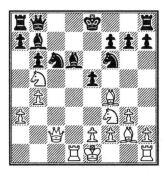

Black to move

Once again he was exploiting his opponent's last move. He would win after 15...♗e7 16 ♗xe5! (16...♘xe5 17 ♘c7+).

Little better is 15...exf4 16 ♘xd6+ and 17 ♘xb7.

The only way to reach a competitive middlegame was **15...0-0!**.

Then **16 ♘xd6 exf4** isn't nearly as bad for Black as in the previous note because of his potential tactics.

For example, 17 ♘xb7 ♕xb7 18 ♘d4 appears to win material.

But Black's knight is not pinned (18...♘xd4! 19 ♗xb7 ♘xc2+). The same goes for 18 ♘e5 ♘xb4!.

Capablanca could have settled for a solid strategic plus with 18 0-0.

White to move

But his chance to get the most out of the g2-c6 pressure could only be realized by **17 ♘h4!**.

There was no good defense to 18 ♘xb7 and ♕xc6.

Black opted for **17...♘d8 18 ♘xb7 ♘xb7** and lost the endgame after **19 ♕c6! fxg3 20 hxg3 ♕e5 21 ♕xb7**.

Was this a combination? Only the most ardent Capablanca fan would claim he foresaw 21 ♕xb7 when he chose 12 ♘b5. It was really an initiative based on exploiting his opponent's previous move. Here's a modern example.

Price – Gormally, Hastings 2019/20

1 e4 c5 2 ♘c3 d6 3 ♘f3 a6 4 d4 cxd4 5 ♘xd4 ♘f6 6 ♗c4 e6 7 a3 ♗e7 8 0-0 0-0 9 ♗e3 ♘c6 10 f4 d5 11 exd5 exd5 12 ♗e2 ♖e8 13 ♗f2

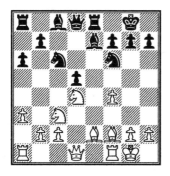

Black to move

65

White's last move anticipated the loss of a pawn from 13...♗xa3 and 14...♖xe3.

But 13 ♗f2 provided other new information to Black. The f4-pawn lost its protection.

He attacked it with **13...♗d6!**.

White may not have liked **14 g3**. But 14 ♕d2 ♕c7! was no better.

It was easy to understand **14...♗h3 15 ♖e1**. Then it seemed that Black had run out of forcing moves.

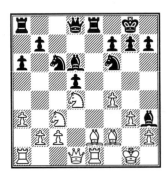

Black to move

He hadn't. He could exploit 15 ♖e1 with **15...♗c5** and a threat of 16...♘xd4 17 ♗xd4 ♕b6!.

This would win after 18 ♗xc5 ♕xc5+ 19 ♔h1 ♕f2 20 ♖g1 d4!.

Or after 20 ♗f1 ♗g4 21 ♗e2 ♖xe2!.

What can White do? There is no escape from 16 ♕d2? ♘e4!.

Only slight better is 16 ♕d3 ♘xd4 17 ♗xd4 ♗f5 18 ♕d2 ♕b6.

And 16 ♘b3 ♗xf2+ 17 ♔xf2 ♕b6+ is over.

The game saw **16 ♘xc6** and **16...♗xf2+ 17 ♔xf2 bxc6**.

White to move

66

The new threat is 18...♕b6+.

There is little respite in 18 ♘a4 ♕c7 (idea: ...♕a7+) 19 b4 ♕a7+ 20 ♘c5 ♘e4+.

White fell back on **18 ♕d4**.

But a move like this virtually shouts for the blockade-breaking **18...c5!**.

Black would win after 19 ♕d2 d4 (or 19...♕b6) and 19 ♕a4 d4 (or 19...c4)

After **19 ♕xc5 d4**, White could not move the knight because of ...♘e4+.

Even 20 ♖ad1 dxc3! 21 ♖xd8 ♘e4+ is lost.

He resigned after **20 ♗f3 dxc3 21 ♖xe8+ ♕xe8 22 ♖e1 ♕d8**.

Mistake Sense

When you face stronger opponents, you are likely to become less careful. You won't expect stronger players to blunder.

Asking "What is wrong with his move?" will seem like a waste of time. As a result, you can let a gross error go unpunished.

You can try to protect yourself against this by using your sense of surprise. This is not an everyday sense of surprise but a specialized one that chess players develop.

Even grandmasters cannot predict every move their opponent will make. When a good player makes a move you didn't expect, it will probably be a good move. He is, after all, a good player.

But good players also make mistakes. This is why a surprise should prompt you to ask, "What is wrong with his move?"

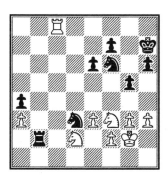

Topalov – Carlsen
Nanjing 2010
White to move

Carlsen expected 32 ♖c4 because it would win the a4-pawn.

He looked for compensating play and weighed 32...e5 and ...e4.

As he waited for White to move, Magnus also considered the possibility of 32 ♖d8.

He was reassured when he saw how 32...♘c5 would prepare ...♘fe4.

Then came a surprise. White played **32 ♖c3**.

Carlsen saw its benefits: It attacks the knight, like 32 ♖d8, but rules out 32...♘c5.

Black to move

Carlsen sensed 32 ♖c3 was an error. He didn't know why.

He looked at 32...♘e1+, so that 33 ♘xe1 ♖xd2.

He carried that further and saw that 34 ♖c4 would win the a4-pawn. But he would be in no danger after 34...♘d5 35 ♔f3 ♖a2, for example.

This explained why 32 ♖c3 might not be good for White. But it didn't explain to Carlsen why he sensed it could be bad.

Then it struck him: **32...♘xf2!** works because of 33 ♔xf2 ♘e4+.

White was suddenly lost. He resigned after **33 ♖c7 ♘2e4**, in view of, for example, 34 ♔g1 ♘xd2 35 ♖xf7+ ♔g8 36 ♖xf6 ♔g7!.

Strategic Downside

Most of the examples we've looked at show how an opponent's last move can be punished by tactics. But more often a faulty last move can be exploited positionally.

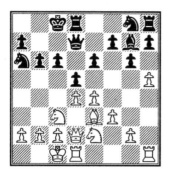

Shulman – Murshed
Dhaka 1999
Black to play

Black made a natural, developing move, **11...♘e7**. He never fully recovered.

The drawback is that it weakens both f6 and h6. White punished it with **12 h6!**, so that 12...♗f6? 13 e5.

He followed with **12...♗f8 13 ♗g5!**.

After 13...♖e8 14 ♗f6 ♖g8 White can increase pressure with 15 ♘f4. That would be followed by ♘h3-g5xh7 or 15...g5 16 ♘d3.

Instead, play went **13...♘c7 14 ♕f4 f5 15 ♕e5! ♖g8 16 ♕f6**.

Black to move

Now 16...♘e8 17 ♕f7 and ♘f4 would show how paralyzed Black's pieces are.

He was lost after **16...dxe4 17 fxe4 fxe4 18 ♘xe4 ♕d5 19 ♘2c3 ♕f5 20 ♖hf1 ♕xf6 21 ♘xf6 ♖h8 22 ♘g4!** in view of 22 ♖f7, 22 ♘e5 or 22 ♖xf8/23 ♗xe7.

In more complex positions, it may take a tactically justified move to punish a positionally flawed move.

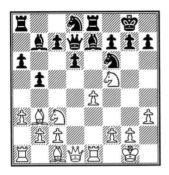

Anand – Shirov
Mainz 2004
Black to move

Black did not want to allow 15 ♘xe7+ . He chose **14...♗f8**.

White saw how this made a threat, 15...♘xe4.

But did it have a drawback?

The only apparent one was that **15 ♗g5!** and 16 ♗xf6! would wreck Black's king protection.

To play 15 ♗g5, White needed more than positional understanding of a bad pawn structure. He needed to calculate a few short tactics.

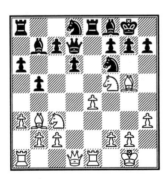

Black to move

First, he saw that 15...♘xe4 now fails to 16 ♕g4!. This would threaten to win the queen (17 ♘h6+) or the knight (17 ♘xe4).

Black could admit the error of 14...♗f8? by playing 15...♗e7.

But it would be hard to recover from the loss of two tempi. For example, 16 ♕d2 ♘e6 17 ♘xe7+ ♕xe7 18 ♘d5.

So, Black forged ahead with **15...♗xe4**.

70

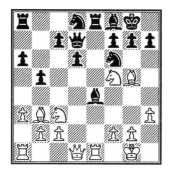

White to move

White won with **16 ♘xe4 ♖xe4 17 ♖xe4** because of 17...♘xe4 18 ♕g4! and, as the game went, **17...♕xf5 18 ♗xf6 ♕xe4 19 ♗d5**.

He probably did not calculate 15 ♗g5 ♗xe4 deeply because he might have found the even stronger 16 ♘h6+! gxh6 17 ♗xf6.

But the takeaway is that it took relatively little calculation to spot the strategic blunder, 14...♗f8?.

Long-Term Dividends

Exploiting the positional drawback of an opponent's last move often means taking advantage of a change in the pawn structure. This can pay strategic dividends that last a long time – because pawn structures last a long time.

Gelfand – Adams
Wijk aan Zee 1994
Black to move

Quick sight tells White he can play ♗xh7. Calculation spoils this by pointing out that he would get insufficient compensation after ...g6! traps the bishop.

71

But ♗xh7 remains stored information for both players. It may work later.

Naturally, Black wanted to rule ♗xh7 out. But 15...g6 would weaken his dark squares and invite 16 ♗h6! ♖fe8 17 ♘e4.

A second way to stop ♗xh7 is 15...h6. But even without a pawn on it, h7 remains a target. Then 16 ♕d2 prepares ♗b1 and ♕c2!.

Black opted for the third way, **15...f5.**

White to move

Does this, too, have a downside? Well, you can talk in text-book terms, about how it makes the e6-bishop "bad." Sounds impressive but it doesn't help White choose his next move.

More useful information is that 15...f5 abandons pawn control of e6. White can translate that into moves: If he doubles his rooks on the e-file he will threaten the e6-bishop.

This plan is easy to execute. After **16 ♗c1!** Black could not stop ♖e2 and ♖de1.

Play went **16...♖ad8 17 ♖e2! ♗f6 18 ♖de1 ♗c8.**

White to move

Black has safeguarded his bishop and found a weak point in White's camp, the d4-pawn. Now 19 &xf5? would allow 19...&xf5 20 ♕xf5 ♘xc3 21 bxc3 &xd4.

But let's ask once more: Is there a drawback to Black's last move?

The answer is: Yes, the d5-knight is underprotected. This prompted **19 &c4!**.

Black has three basic ways to respond. He can trade, 19...♘xc3, advance 19...♘f4 or put one of his knights on e7.

But, guess what, each has a drawback. For example, he would lose a pawn after 19...♘de7? 20 ♘b5! ♕d7 21 &e6!.

He also loses a pawn after 19...♘ce7, if White takes twice on d5, followed by ♕xc7.

Black didn't like 19...♘f4, apparently because of 20 &xf4 ♕xf4 21 ♘d5!.

This left **19...♘xc3 20 bxc3**.

Then Black had to stop ♘g5 with **20...h6**.

White to move

It may not look like much has happened since 15...f5, but White's domination of the e-file matters. With 21 &e6 or 21 &a2 followed by ♘e5 or d4-d5 he would he headed to a strategic victory.

All Answers Lead To ...

As we saw in the last chapter, the best move can often be found by asking other checklist questions. "What is wrong with his move?" may just be the most efficient one.

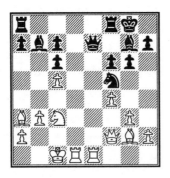

Nepomniachtchi – Tomashevsky
Moscow 2016
Black to move

The only move to save Black's attacked queen is **19...♕f7**.

If White asks "What are the tactical ideas?" he will get the same answer he would to "What is wrong with 19...♕f7?"

Black's queen and king are lined up on a diagonal that is easily seized, by **20 ♗f1!** and the crushing **♗c4**.

Black resigned after **20...♖fd8 21 ♖xd8+ ♖xd8 22 ♗c4 ♖d5 23 ♕e2**.

A checklist question we will visit later is "How can I improve my pieces?" You might get the correct answer faster by focusing once again on your opponent's last move.

Karpov – Hort, Budapest 1973

1 e4 e6 2 d4 d5 3 ♘d2 ♘f6 4 e5 ♘fd7 5 c3 c5 6 ♗d3 ♘c6 7 ♘e2 ♕b6 8 ♘f3 cxd4 9 cxd4 f6 10 exf6 ♘xf6 11 0-0 ♗d6 12 ♘c3 0-0 13 ♗e3 ♕d8

White to move

There are general-principle moves to consider, such as 14 ♖c1 and 14 ♖e1. But to Anatoly Karpov, Black's last move recommended **14 ♗g5**.

Why? Because once Black retreated his queen, Karpov no longer needed the bishop to protect his d4-pawn. Pinning the f6-knight made better use of it.

In addition, Karpov saw a favorable maneuver, ♗h4-g3!. It is a good positional idea – to trade off Black's good bishop – that had been stored in his consciousness since 11…♗d6.

But he couldn't use it when the queen was still on b6 because of …♕xb2!.

Black got out of the pin on his f6-knight with **14…♗d7 15 ♖e1 ♕b8**.

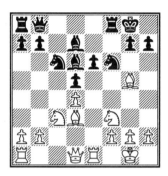

White to move

What does Black threaten? It should not take long to see that 16…♘g4! attacks the h2-pawn.

If White responds 17 h3? he allows 17…♗h2+ 18 ♔f1 ♘xf2! so that 19 ♔xf2 ♕g3+ 20 ♔f1 ♕xg5.

He can also lose after 17 g3 h6 18 ♗d2? ♘xd4! 19 ♘xd4 ♘xf2.

Those nightmares were more than enough reason for Karpov to continue **16 ♗h4** with the idea of ♗g3.

There followed **16…a6 17 ♖c1 b5 18 ♗b1 ♗f4 19 ♗g3! ♗xg3 20 hxg3 ♕b6 21 ♘e2**.

Black to move

Let's assess: The bishop trade created holes on c5 and e5 and magnified the inferiority of Black's bad bishop.

White can improve his winning chances with ♘f4, ♛d3 and, if allowed, ♘g5 or ♘e5.

Black's constructive moves are more or less limited to doubling rooks on the c-file. His position would be going downhill after 21...♖ac8 22 ♛d3 ♖c7 23 ♖cd1 ♖fc8 24 ♘f4, for example.

He gambled on **21...♖ae8 22 ♘f4 ♘xd4** and would have been in bad shape after 23 ♘xd4 e5 24 ♘xd5 ♘xd5 25 ♘f3.

But ...

And it is an important "but." There are often positions in which two checklist questions will point you in different directions. You can pay too much attention to one at the expense of the other.

For example, "What does he threaten?" may cause you to focus on the positive side of an opponent's move and overlook its downside. Here is how 12-year-old Garry Kasparov was misled by this.

Kasparov – Yermolinsky, Baku 1975

1 e4 ♘f6 2 e5 ♘d5 3 d4 d6 4 ♘f3 ♗g4 5 ♗e2 e6 6 0-0 ♗e7 7 h3 ♗h5 8 c4 ♘b6 9 exd6 cxd6 10 ♘bd2 0-0 11 b3 ♘c6 12 ♗b2 ♗f6 13 a3 d5 14 c5 ♘c8 15 b4 a6 16 ♖c1 ♘8e7

White to move

This was a book opening until Black's 14th move, rather than 14...♘d7.

Kasparov figured out the point of his knight maneuver. Black intended a triple attack on the d4-pawn after ...♘f5.

So, Kasparov chose **17 ♘b3??**. Only after the game did he realize that **16...♘8e7??** was a blunder. It should have lost a piece to 17 g4! ♗g6 18 g5.

Dumbing Down ...

One final point about "What is wrong with his move?"

If nothing occurs to you – because his move doesn't weaken a pawn, abandon control of a key square, or reduce protection of a piece – ask yourself a stupid question.

Could his move be a gross blunder? Does it allow mate in one move? Does it put his queen en prise?

Kasimdzhanov – Kasparov, Batumi 2001

1 d4 ♞f6 2 c4 e6 3 g3 c5 4 d5 exd5 5 cxd5 b5 6 ♗g2 d6 7 b4 ♞bd7 8 bxc5 dxc5 9 ♞h3 ♗d6 10 0-0??

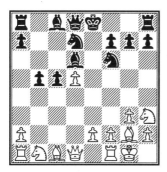

Black to move

There didn't seem to be any strategic disadvantage to exploit. Kasparov played 10...0-0??. How long does it take you to find an improvement?

What To Remember

Your opponent's last move is the best clue to finding your best reply to it. Once he moves you should determine whether it changes the position significantly and what its drawbacks may be.

The drawback may be tactical and be punishable tactically, even by an "impossible" move you would not normally consider. Or it may be a positional concession that can be exploited by a simple positional move or tactically justified ones.

Initiatives are created out of a series of moves that exploit each of the opponent's previous moves. When you ask "What is wrong with his last move?" be sure to see if it is a blunder.

Quiz

25.

Keres – Spassky
Gothenburg 1955
Black to move

White met the threat of 30 ♖xf6 with **29...♘6d7**. What is wrong with his move?

26.

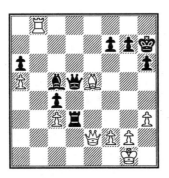

Svidler – Carlsen
London 2013
White to move

White's **33 ♕h5** threatened 34 ♕f5+ and mate. But it handed Black a tactic. Which?

27.

Pigusov – Savon
Moscow 1989
Black to move

Black chose **15...b5**. What is the drawback?

28.

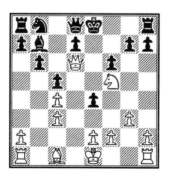

Cordes – Miles
Bad Wörishofen 1985
Black to move

Black played **12...g6**. What did he overlook?

29.

Kindermann – W. Schmidt
Warsaw 1983
Black to move

Black defended his e-pawn with **22...♗d6**. Why is this wrong?

30.

Benjamin – Seirawan
Los Angeles 1991
Black to move

Black played **27...♛b4**. How can this be a mistake?

31.

Romanishin – Lputian, Kiev 1984

1 c4 e6 2 ♘c3 d5 3 d4 c5 4 ♗e3

Black to move

White wants to clarify the center (4...♘c6 5 ♘f3 cxd4 6 ♘xd4). Can this be an error?

32.

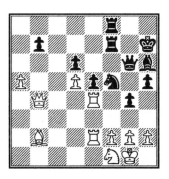

X3D Fritz – Kasparov
New York 2003
Black to play

Why did **32...♖g7?** deserve a question mark?

33.

Cori – So
Internet 2020
White to move

How could **29 ♔h2** be an error?

34.

Tukmakov – Kochiev
Ashgabat 1978
Black to move

Black's **24...♖xa2** gave White a tactical idea. What?

35.

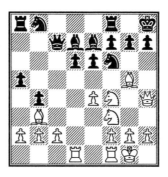

Kasparov – Gelfand
Linares 1993
Black to move

Why was **17...♗b5** wrong?

36.

Vachier-Lagrave – So
Internet 2020
White to move

White chose **45 ♗g7** so that 45...h5 46 ♗f6 or 45...♔xh4 46 ♗xh6 blockades. What was wrong with this?

37.

Larsen – Tal
Bugojno 1984
White to move

Black threatens 28...♘f3+. White chose **29 ♗xd4** so that 29...♘f3+?? 30 ♕xf3! ♕xf3 31 ♖xg7+ ♔f8 32 ♖f1. Was this right?

38.

Short – J. Polgar
Buenos Aires 2001
White to move

White targeted f6 with **36 ♘g4.** He saw 36...♗h5? 37 ♘xf6!. What did he miss?

39.

Taimanov – Karaklajić
Leningrad 1957
Black to move

White has just captured on e4. Was **14...dxe4** best?

40.

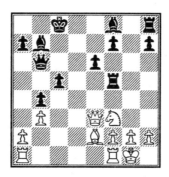

Korchnoi – Ivanchuk
Lvov 2000
White to move

To anticipate ...♖g8 and ...♕c6, White chose **19 ♘e5**, with the idea of 20 ♗f3. How is this punished?

41.

Karpov – Korchnoi
Zürich 2006
White to move

In a blitz battle of old rivals Black met **56 ♕d2** with **56...♖f5** and lost. What did he overlook?

Chapter Four:
What Is The Principled Move?

When Belle, the pioneering chess engine, was improved with new hardware, its programmer believed it would make a huge jump in rating strength, from 1900 to 2400.

The new Belle was better, but not that much better. The programmer investigated and found that it was indeed 500 points stronger – in tactical skill. But Belle had not improved nearly as much in the other chess skills.

Humans experience something similar. As you get better at spotting pins, skewers and x-ray attacks, your overall chess ability grows. But you eventually run into a law of diminishing returns. Your results improve, but to a much lesser degree.

To reach the next skill level faster, you need to fine-tune the way you evaluate candidate moves. You still need to consider tactics but as a supporting actor, not as the featured performer.

Suetin – Borisenko
Kiev 1954
White to move

Tactics seem to be available to Black, but not White. Black threatens to capture the c2-pawn. If White defends it with 26 ♘b4, he would be in trouble after 26...f5!.

For instance, 27 gxf5 ♖xf5 and ...♘f3+. Or 27 ♕xe7+ ♖f7 28 ♕xd8 ♘f3+.

Instead of agonizing over scenarios like this, White should recall the general principles he learned as a beginner. Everyone knows them: Put your bishops on open diagonals, find outposts for your knights and so on.

Let's take another look at the diagram. Suppose there were no Black threats and White had to rely purely on general principles. What other moves should White consider?

A prime candidate is **26 ♖ad1**. It develops a rook on an open file. No deep strategy here.

To play it White needs a little calculation. The news is good. First, he would see that 26...♘xc2? loses the knight to 27 ♘b4!.

Second, 26...♖xc2? also drops material, to 27 ♘e5! (27...♘e2+ 28 ♔f1).

Black to move

Once White appreciates this, the position suddenly looks different. He is the one doing the threatening, with 27 ♘e5 and ♖xd4.

Black's knight has become a liability, not a strength. He would be worse after 26...♘e6 27 ♘f4! ♕c7 28 ♘xe6+.

Instead, he played **26...♘c6?** and was losing after **27 ♘c5! ♕e8 28 ♘d7** or 27...♕c7 28 ♖d7.

It seems like a magical transformation from the unpromising White position in the first diagram. But all that changed was that White looked at the most principle-based move.

Why Can't I?

A master can spend minutes considering a move like 26 ♖ad1. It is not because it took that long to remember that rooks should be developed on open files.

He takes time because he is trying to give himself a kind of permission: "I want to play this candidate because it is the principled move. Why *can't* I play it?"

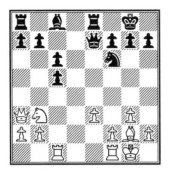

Ståhlberg – Keres
Gothenburg 1938
Black to move

White is attacking the c5-pawn three times. Black can't defend it with enough pieces. But if he uses a pawn, 16...b6, he allows 17 ♗xc6.

How should Black spend his thinking time? One way is to concentrate on the consequences of a White capture on c5. He would see 16...♗f5 17 ♘xc5, for example, is slightly worse for him.

He can live with that. After all, he is Black, playing a good opponent, and should not expect equality when the opening ends.

But before accepting this, he should take a fresh look at the diagrammed position. What is the principled move?

Of course, it is **16...b6**. It is too desirable from a positional point of view – solidifying the pawn structure – to reject without calculating **17 ♗xc6** further.

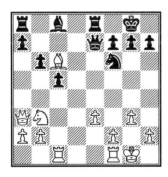

Black to move

Paul Keres convinced himself to play 16...b6 after he calculated **17...♗b7**.

He felt he would have sufficient compensation for the Exchange after 18 ♗xe8 ♖xe8.

Then he would threaten mate with 19...♕e4. He could generate play after 19 ♖ce1 ♘e4. (He might have done even better with 17...♗h3 18 ♗xe8 ♖xe8.)

In any case, White mistrusted 18 ♗xe8. He traded bishops, **18 ♗xb7 ♕xb7**.

White to move

But the pawn structure favored Black's better-placed pieces. He won after **19 ♕a4 ♖ad8 20 ♖fd1 ♘e4** (20...♕f3!) **21 ♘d2 ♘g5! 22 ♕g4 ♖xd2! 23 ♕xg5 ♕d7 24 ♖xd2 ♕xd2**.

Short Tactics

A beginner learns to say "yes" to a candidate move before he learns to say "no." This is natural and good.

He is improving when he can say "I want to play this move and I can explain why."

Then he learns more about tactics. He finds himself adding, "But I can't play it."

To advance further, he has to learn how to be as certain that the move is tactically sound as he is that it is positionally good. This may mean looking only two or three moves into the future.

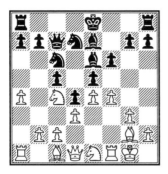

Piket – Timman
Amsterdam 1996
White to move

White is cramped by the pawn structure. General principles indicate a trade of a minor pieces, especially of his g2-bishop, should help him.

This gives White a strategy. He needs to check it: What happens after 12 ♗f3 and 13 ♗g4 ?

The answer he may get is 12...0-0-0 13 ♗g4 ♗xc4!. Then 14 dxc4 exf4 could turn out well. But it might turn out badly. It is too unclear to tell without much deeper calculation.

But the basic idea of trading bishops makes such solid positional sense that White should try to find another way to execute it. He found **12 ♗h3!**.

Black to move

It is based on a simple tactic, 12...♗xh3 13 ♕h5+ and ♕xh3.

Offering the bishop trade in one move rather than two would leave White virtually a tempo ahead of what he looked at earlier: Compare 12 ♗h3 ♗xc4 13 dxc4 with 12 ♗f3 0-0-0 13 ♗g4 ♗xc4 13 dxc4.

In reply to 12 ♗h3, Black can be guided by general principles, too. But if he keeps his better bishop with 12...♗f7 he finds short tactics that favor White after 13 ♕g4!.

This threatens ♕xg7 and might make ♕xd7+ favorable.

In the end, Black accepted the consequences of **12...♗xh3 13 ♕h5+ g6 14 ♕xh3.**

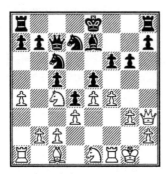

Black to move

Those consequences are clear. White exposed e6 and h6 as weakened squares.

He would have the upper hand after 14...0-0-0 15 fxe5 fxe5 16 ♗h6! because of his control of the f-file. Or he would control a key diagonal after 15...♘xe5 16 ♘xe5 ♕xe5 17 ♗f4.

Play went **14...♘b6 15 fxe5! fxe5**, and now 16 ♘xb6 followed by ♕e6 and ♗h6 would have been powerful.

Evolutionary and Revolutionary

Examples like that can lead to an oversimplification: "Strategy is making plans. Tactics is executing the plans."

In truth, many plans are carried out with a minimum of tactics. Aron Nimzovich described this method as the "evolutionary" way. It is based on maneuvering, such as ♗g2-f3-g4 in the last example.

There is often a faster method, what Nimzovich called the "revolutionary" way.

Blatny – Salai, Stary Smokovec 1990

1 ♘f3 f5 2 d3 d5 3 c4 e6 4 cxd5 exd5 5 g3 ♘f6 6 ♗g2 ♗d6 7 0-0 0-0 8 ♘c3 c6

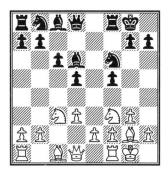

White to move

Black planned a middlegame based on his light-square center pawns. Given time, he will develop smoothly behind them, for example, with …♘a6-c5 and …b6/…♗b7.

General principles indicate e2-e4 could blow up Black's center before he is ready. White can prepare the pawn push with 9 ♕c2 or 9 ♖e1.

This is the evolutionary method. It turns out well after, for instance, 9 ♕c2 ♘a6 10 e4 fxe4 11 dxe4 dxe4 12 ♘xe4 ♘xe4 13 ♕xe4.

But if e2-e4 is the best plan, why can't it be played immediately? When White asks "Why can't I?" he finds the pawn sacrifice **9 e4!**.

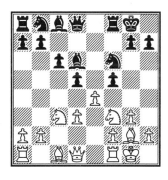

Black to move

To justify 9 e4, he would look at **9…dxe4 10 dxe4** and 10…♘xe4 11 ♘xe4 fxe4.

He would see 12 ♘g5 and ♘xe4 would regain the pawn with a nice game.

If he rechecked this, he might see 12 ♕b3+! ♔h8 13 ♘g5 is even better.

Note the revolutionary 9 e4 method is justified by about the same amount of calculation as the evolutionary 9 ♕c2.

What makes 9 e4 more desirable is that it offered chances for a greater edge (in the 12 ♕b3+ line) or as the game went, **10...fxe4 11 ♘g5.**

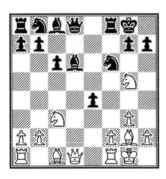

Black to move

Now 11...♗g4? 12 ♕b3+ is clearly bad for Black and illustrates how 9 e4 saved a tempo compared with 9 ♕c2.

In addition, White could enjoy the middlegame after 11...♘a6 12 ♘cxe4.

Play went **11...♕e7? 12 ♘cxe4**. Black was in serious trouble, as 12...♘d5 13 ♖e1 indicates.

Not much better was **12...♘xe4 13 ♗xe4!**. Then 13...h6 14 ♗g6! would set up a winning 15 ♕b3+ (and 14...hxg5?? 15 ♕h5 is a mate).

After **13...♗f5**, White might have won quickly with 14 ♕d3 or 14 ♗xf5 ♖xf5 15 ♕c2.

But **14 ♖e1 ♕d7 15 ♕b3+ ♔h8 16 ♖d1!** was nearly as good because of the pin on the d-file.

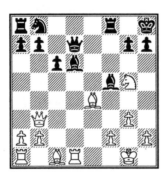

Black to move

There was no defense, e.g. 16...h6 17 ♗f4 hxg5 18 ♗xd6.

Black resigned after **16...♗g4? 17 ♗f4! ♗xd1 18 ♖xd1**.

Making Desirable Work

Masters often talk about "positional understanding." This sounds like a profound and mysterious skill that takes years to achieve.

But in many cases positional understanding is just recognizing the most principled candidate move. The more desirable a move is from a positional viewpoint, the more you should try to make it work.

"Make it work" is master jargon. This means to calculate the consequences of a move until you feel confident playing it.

Mikhalevski – I. Sokolov
Leeuwarden 1994
Black to move

A master doesn't have to ask himself whether **13...c5** would be desirable.

Of course, it is: It frees the b7-bishop and enables the a6-knight and c8-rook to play the middlegame.

Tactics make 13...c5 work – 14 dxc5?? is bad because the a1-rook is hanging after 14...♘xe4.

The d4-pawn is also pinned after 14 bxc5 ♘xe4 15 ♗xe4 ♘xc5.

But **14 ♘xc5!** is a tougher nut to crack.

Black had compensation after **14...♗xf3 15 gxf3 e5!**.

White to move

Now 16 dxe5 ♘d7 would be good for him (17 ♗e2 ♘axc5 and 17 f4? ♘axc5 18 bxc5 ♖xc5).

The position became double-edged after **16 ♗xb5 ♘c7 17 ♗d3 exd4 18 e4 axb4 19 axb4 ♘h5**.

Black won after **20 ♕b3 ♕f6 21 ♔e2 ♘e6! 22 ♘d7 ♘ef4+ 23 ♔d1 ♕g5** (24 ♘xf8? ♕g2!).

Thematic

Another term that masters like to use is "thematic." This describes a move that follows a strategic theme in certain common pawn structures.

One thematic move is …d5 in the Hedgehog pawn formation. The Hedgehog features Black pawns on d6 and e6 that are restricted by White pawns on c4 and e4. It was discredited for decades because White enjoys much more space.

This view changed when Black began to try …d5 as a sacrifice. A new strategic theme was born.

Estevez – Larsen
Leningrad 1973
Black to move

White's last move was 16 f3. It strengthened his e4-pawn.

But there was a downside. It made **16...d5** more desirable.

Why is it desirable? Because now Black has two diagonals, c5-g1 and d6-h2, on which to mount threats with his bishop.

In addition, his e8-rook and his b7-bishop will get into the game after **17 exd5** (or 17 cxd5) **exd5**.

White to move

Black couldn't be sure he would get the pawn back when he played 16...d5!.

But he liked what he saw when he calculated continuations such as 18 ♘xd5 ♗xd5! 19 cxd5 ♗c5 20 ♕d2 ♗d6.

Post-game analysis showed he would have had compensation for his sacrificed material after 21 f4 ♘e4! or 21 g3 ♗xg3!.

The same goes for 21 h3 ♘h5!, with the idea of ...♗h2+/...♘g3+.

This was enough to scare White into declining the pawn. He chose **18 ♗f4** and then **18...♕a7 19 ♔h1? ♗c5! 20 ♕d2**.

Black to move

97

The upshot is Black was the one with more operating space after **20...dxc4! 21 ♗xc4 b5 22 ♗b3 ♘e5**, threatening 23...♘xf3! (24 gxf3 ♗xf3+).

White wasn't ready to play the humble 23 ♘e1 and resigned after **23 ♘d5? ♗xd5 24 ♗xd5 ♖ad8 25 ♘e3 ♘c4**.

Fusion

One more term masters use is "positional play." When asked what it means, masters give different answers. Among them: It means "maneuvering," or "gradually improving the position," or "accumulating small advantages" or simply "not tactical."

None of the definitions explain what happens in games like the following.

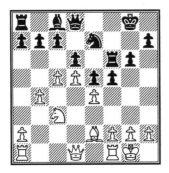

Taimanov – Petrosian
Vilnius 1958
White to move

One of the last checklist questions we will consider is "Will my position get better?" – that is, with routine, principled moves.

Here this could mean 17 ♖c1. This move eyes the c7 square, after cxd6 and ♘b5. A double-edged struggle on the queenside could follow 17...a5.

But there are subtle features of the position that pointed White in a different direction. Black is behind in development and his knight and f6-rook are somewhat misplaced.

There is no way to exploit this as long as the center is closed. This made **17 f4!** positionally desirable. White wants to blow open the center with 18 fxe5 dxe5 19 ♗c4.

The only continuation that required more than casual calculation by White was 17...fxe4 18 fxe5!.

98

After the forced trade of rooks, 18...♖xf1+ 19 ♗xf1 (or 19 ♕xf1), he would favorably regain his pawn, 19...dxe5 20 ♗c4! and ♘xe4.

The great defender Tigran Petrosian tried **17...exf4**. He saw that White would not get his pawn back quickly with 18 exf5? ♖xf5.

Petrosian's main point was that 18 ♖xf4 g5! would keep the center and kingside relatively closed and allow him to coordinate his pieces after 19 ♖f1 f4! and ...♘g6.

White to move

White took advantage of this last move with **18 ♕d4!**.

By attacking the misplaced rook he won time to continue **18...♖f7 19 e5!**.

Now the ...g5/...♘g6 idea is too slow. For instance, 19...g5 20 ♗h5 ♖g7 21 ♖ae1 ♘g6 and now 22 exd6 cxd6 23 ♘b5!.

Computers often like the looks of tactical, unprincipled continuations such as 19...dxc5 20 bxc5 ♘c6 21 ♕xf4 g5 and 22 ♕g3? f4!.

But when they look further, at 22 ♕d2! ♘xe5 23 ♖ae1, they appreciate how badly off Black would be.

Instead, Petrosian chose **19...dxe5 20 ♕xe5 g5**.

White to move

It was a rare sight to see him outplayed by simple, principled moves, **21 ♗c4! ♘g6 22 ♕d4**.

He rejected the lost endgame of 22...♕f6 23 ♕xf6 ♖xf6 24 ♘b5 and lost after **22...♖g7 23 d6+ ♔f8 24 ♖fe1 cxd6 25 ♘b5 d5 26 ♘d6**.

How many of White's moves could be called "maneuvering" or "gradually improving the position"? Very few. How many were based on tactics? Most.

Emanuel Lasker said positional play and tactics needed to be "fused" into a "harmonious unity." When he wrote this, a century ago, it was controversial. Players – and moves – were described then as either tactical or positional. Today we know that good strategists are good tacticians. They could not be otherwise.

Work Harder

When you play over an impressive game by one of the classic strategists – such as José Capablanca, Anatoly Karpov or Vishy Anand – you may find yourself saying:

"I know his moves looked right. After all, I know general principles. But I couldn't see myself playing some of these moves. They seemed to fail tactically."

When you are attracted to a particular move but disappointed when you begin calculating its consequences, the best policy is: Look a little further. It may take consideration of one additional move to justify your good idea.

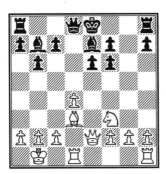

Gipslis – Darznieks
Latvian Championship 1962
White to move

White noticed 13 d5 because it is another thematic move. It often succeeds in this and similar pawn structures.

White was attracted to it because he would enjoy a large positional advantage if he can continue dxe6.

He would also have a big edge after 13...e5 because he can exploit the light squares at f5 and h5, with 14 ♘h4 and ♘f5/♕h5, for example.

When he began calculating, it was easy to see that 13...♕xd5? would drop the queen to 14 ♗b5+.

But figuring out what to do after 13...♗xd5 was harder. White's compensation for a pawn would be nebulous after 14 c4 ♗xf3 15 ♕xf3, for example.

Before giving up on 13 d5 ♗xd5, White looked further. To justify it, he needed a forcing move, like 14 c4.

He found 14 ♗b5+!. This would improve the c2-c4 idea (14...♔f8 15 c4 and wins).

Armed with this confidence, White played **13 d5!**.

Black could see the same 13...♗xd5 14 ♗b5+ as White. He answered **13...exd5**.

White to move

When he considered 13 d5, White realized how 13...exd5 could be answered by **14 ♘d4!**.

This is a general-principle move – occupy the center with knights. It enhances his tactical ideas, such as 15 ♖he1 and ♘f5/♘xe7.

It also prepares ♗b5+ and/or ♘f5, in coordination with ♕h5. For example, 15 ♕h5 c5? 16 ♗b5+ ♔f8 17 ♕h6+ ♔g8 18 ♖d3 and ♖g3 mate.

Black's chances of safely reaching a middlegame depended on stopping ♕h5 with 14...h5. But those chances would be slim after 15 ♗b5+ ♔f8 16 ♕f3, followed by ♖he1 and ♘f5.

Black made it easy with **14...c5? 15 ♘f5 ♗c8 16 ♗b5+ ♔f8** because White found **17 ♖xd5! ♕c7 18 ♖d7! resigns**.

Maybe

In many positions, even a grandmaster cannot calculate far enough to be sure that a positionally desirable move is sound or not. The best he can get is a "maybe."

Some players, who are like Mikhail Tal, enjoy playing "maybe" moves. Others, who are like Bobby Fischer, do not. Fischer always preferred a solid move he knew would improve his position over a move that might provide much more but could not be easily justified.

Fischer – Ault, New York 1958-1959

1 e4 d6 2 d4 ♘f6 3 ♘c3 g6 4 ♗g5 ♗g7 5 ♕d2 ♘bd7 6 0-0-0 e5 7 dxe5 dxe5 8 ♘f3 h6 9 ♗h4 g5 10 ♗g3 ♕e7 11 h4! g4

White to move

Fischer's last move is a standard positional idea, what the Russians call a "priyome." Its goal is to exploit Black's kingside weaknesses after **12 ♘h2**, with f2-f3.

Fischer enjoyed a modest edge after **12...c6 13 f3 h5 14 ♔b1 ♗h6 15 ♕f2** and won a back-and-forth game.

After it was over, it was pointed out **12 ♘xe5!** was sound (12...♘xe5 13 ♗xe5 ♕xe5?? 14 ♕d8 mate).

But this gets complicated after 13...♘xe4!, instead of 13...♕xe5.

Fischer could have investigated **14 ♘xe4 ♗xe5 15 ♕e3**.

And, if necessary, he could have calculated a queen sacrifice, **14 ♗xg7!! ♘xd2 15 ♘d5**.

What might have been

White temporarily has only one piece as compensation. But his attack is overwhelming after 15...♕c5 16 ♖xd2.

But it wasn't necessary. Fischer was certain of a slight advantage after 12 ♘h2. He couldn't be certain about 12 ♘xe5 without a lot of calculation.

Fischer faced a similar decision five years later in a game with Pal Benko. He could have sacrificed his queen for two minor pieces, again on the 14th move. But he wasn't sure it worked. He chose a simple alternative that guaranteed a small but certain advantage. He went on to force mate with a stunning rook sacrifice in what is remembered as one of his greatest victories.

Psychological Punch

You know a surprise tactical shot by your opponent can pack a psychological punch. But so can an unexpected positional move. The shock value of an unanticipated pawn push helped decide a world championship match with this game.

Anand – Kasparov
World Championship match,
New York 1995
Black to move

The pawn structure tends to favor White. Why? Because after he castles he can use his heavy pieces to pound at the e7-pawn, the most vulnerable target on the board.

But **18...e5!** tossed that prospect out the window.

If White lets the new pawn structure stand, he would have no meaningful pressure on the e-file or good alternative plan.

Instead, Black would have a choice of favorable plans, such as preparing ...f5 or offering an endgame with ...♛b4.

Reeling from the surprise, Vishy Anand played **19 dxe6?** and had to deal with **19...d5!**.

White to move

This is justified by small tactics – 20 ♝xd5? ♜fd8 and Black wins the pinned bishop (21 c4 fxe6).

Anand had to settle for **20 ♝e2**, and his disadvantage grew quickly: **20...c4 21 c3 ♜ce8 22 bxc4 ♜xe6**.

The shortest world championship loss in memory ended with **23 ♔f1 ♜fe8 24 ♝d3 dxc4 25 ♝xc4 ♞e4 White resigns**.

Unprincipled

Let's face it: Often the first move you consider playing is one that you know is suspicious. You know this because it clearly violates general principles. But you are strangely attracted to it, at least for a moment.

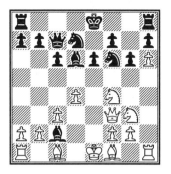

Hess – Postny
Ningbo 2011
White to move

"I momentarily entertained the idea of 13 ♔d2??," White recalled.

This attacks the c2-bishop. Then 13...♗e4 14 ♘xe4 leads to a good middlegame (14...♗xf4+ 15 ♔c2 or 14...♘xe4+ 15 ♕xe4 ♗xf4+ 16 ♔c2).

But White quickly saw 13...♗a4 makes his king look stupid on d2. Black would strongly threaten ...♗xf4+. (White played 13 ♗d3 and eventually won.)

Quite a different thought path is this: You find yourself in a position in which every natural candidate has a drawback. By process of elimination you find yourself considering a principle-challenged move.

Yuferov – Chepukaitis, St. Petersburg 1996

1 d4 g6 2 e4 ♗g7 3 ♘f3 d6 4 ♘c3 a6 5 a4 b6 6 h3 e6 7 ♗g5 ♘e7 8 ♕d2 h6 9 ♗f4 ♗b7 10 ♗e2 ♘d7 11 ♖d1

Black to move

Black's irregular opening has reached an apparent dead end. The most principled move, 11...0-0?, allows 12 ♗xh6.

Instead, he can try to simplify the center with 11...♘f6 12 ♗d3 d5 so that 13 e5 ♘e4.

But general principles suggest 13 exd5 would favor White's better development. This is borne out by 13...♘exd5 14 ♘xd5 ♘xd5 15 ♗e5 and so on.

Black played **11...g5!**. It looks desperate, but it was the best move.

After **12 ♗e3**, Black would have had good play with 12...♘f6 13 ♗d3 ♘g6 and ...0-0.

But **12...f5!** made more sense, both tactically (13...f4!) and positionally.

White to move

Amateurs would be ridiculed for advancing pawns like this before they had castled. But the threat of 13...f4 is hard to meet. And when they conflict, tactics trump principles.

White continued to play natural moves, **13 exf5 ♘xf5 14 ♕d3**.

But after **14...0-0** Black had seized the upper hand. He was ready to crumple what was left of White's model center with 15...c5.

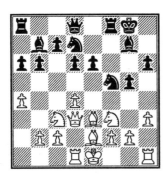

White to move

Black's advantage was obvious after **15 ♗c1 c5 16 dxc5 ♘xc5 17 ♕c4 ♖c8**.

He went on to win after **18 h4 ♗xf3 19 gxf3 ♘xh4 20 ♕g4 ♘g6 21 ♘e4 ♘e5**.

What to Remember

Tactics and general principles are factors in almost all move-selection decisions. The two conflict in some positions and complement one another in others. When they conflict, tactics have the final say. But you should try to fuse the two to find the best move.

If you are attracted to a move based on general principles, don't give up on it because a quick calculation is disappointing. And if you are attracted to a move that contradicts principles, calculate further.

Quiz

42.

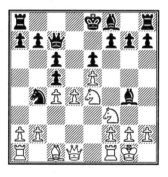

Carlsen – Nataf
Reykjavik 2004
Black to move

Tempting is 10...♗f5 or 10...cxd4, so that 11 ♕xd4 ♗xf3. Is there a better move?

43.

Naiditsch – Caruana
Karlsruhle 2017
White to move

White's **14 ♕b4** threatened 15 ♘b6, e.g. 14...♖b8 15 ♘c5. What did he misjudge?

44.

Sunye Neto – Ashley
New York 1997
Black to move

How should White respond to **15...♘a5** ?

45.

Howell – Ivanchuk
Groningen 1986-7
Black to move

There are problems with 19...♗f6 20 ♕f5!, 19...♗d6 20 ♕h3! and 19...♖fe8 20 b5 ♕b6 21 ♗e3. What else is there?

46.

Topalov – J. Polgar
Las Palmas 1994
White to move

Does Black's threat of ...♗xb2 win time for 10...d6 ?

47.

Short – Kasparov
Amsterdam 1996
Black to move

Black chose **20…h5**. Was this right?

48.

A. Zaitsev – Rashkovsky
Kuibyshev 1970
White to move

What should White do?

49.

Evans – Fischer
New York 1965
Black to move

Centralizing with 20...♘d5 is good. Are there principled alternatives?

50. Reshevsky – Levin, New York 1942

1 d4 ♘f6 2 c4 e6 3 ♘c3 ♗b4 4 a3 ♗xc3+ 5 bxc3 c5 6 e3 0-0 7 ♗d3 d5 8 cxd5 ♕xd5 9 ♘f3 b6 10 ♕e2 ♗b7

White to move

Modern masters play 11 0-0. Is this best?

51. Korchnoi – Fischer, Sousse 1967

1 ♘f3 c5 2 c4 ♘c6 3 ♘c3 g6 4 e3 ♗g7 5 d4 d6 6 d5 ♘e5 7 ♘d2 f5 8 ♗e2 ♘f6 9 h3 0-0 10 f4 ♘f7 11 g4 e5 12. dxe6 ♗xe6 13 g5 ♘e8 14 ♗f3 ♖b8

Was there a better policy for Black than 14...♖b8?

15 a4 ♘c7 16 ♖a3

Black to move

Now what should he do?

52.

Hertneck – Grooten
Salzburg 2004
White to move

White deserves more than 12 ♘b3 ♗e7 13 ♗f4 ♘e5. How does he get it?

53.

Browne – Hulak
Wijk aan Zee 1983
White to move

Black's last move, 15...♕e7, was designed to slow the minority attack (16 b5 ♗xa3). What should White do?

54.

Oll – Iailian
Moscow 1989
White to move

White's best move is based on a distant fork. Which?

55.

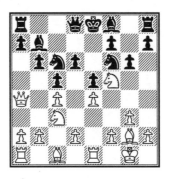

Vaganian – Minasian
Moscow 1991
White to move

How can White use his lead in development?

56.

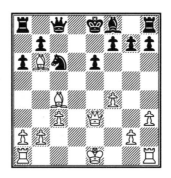

Blatny – Ljubojević
Antwerp 1994
White to move

The line-opening 18 f5 allows 18...♘e7. This threatens 19...♕xc4 as well as 19...♘xf5. What should White do?

57.

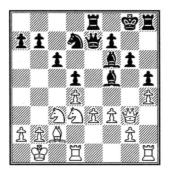

Korchnoi – Bilek
Hamburg 1965
White to move

What is White's most promising positional idea? What is the evolutionary method of carrying it out and what is the revolutionary method? Which is best?

Chapter Five:
What Is His Weakest Point?

One of the surest signs that you are improving at chess is when you can comfortably think well beyond the next move. You foresee something to do in the next two, three or four moves.

That "something" usually means threatening a weak point in your opponent's position. Ideally, it is the weakest point.

Karjakin – Gelfand, World Cup 2009

1 e4 e5 2 ♗c4 ♘f6 3 d3 ♘c6 4 ♘f3 ♗e7 5 0-0 0-0 6 ♗b3 d5 7 exd5 ♘xd5 8 h3 a5 9 a4 ♘d4 10 ♘xd4 exd4 11 ♖e1

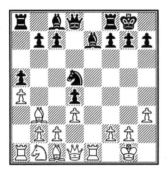

Black to move

No obvious tactical idea stands out, for either player. Principled moves for Black include 11...♖e8 and 11...♗e6.

But when Black noticed **11...♖a6!** "I understood it had to be played!" he said afterward.

What attracted him was how vulnerable the square g2 would be after ...♖g6. This is long-term thinking. In other words, a plan:

It takes two moves to get the a8-rook to g6. It takes one more, by his knight or his c8-bishop, before he can threaten to capture on g2.

White to move

Black exaggerated when he said he "had" to play 11...♖a6 as soon as he noticed it. What he really had to do was make it work. That is, he had to justify the loss of a piece, 12 ♗xd5 ♕xd5 13 ♖xe7.

Black found it would "work" because 13...♖g6! then threatens ...♕xg2 mate. He wins after 14 ♕f1? ♗xh3, for example.

There wasn't much else Black really needed to calculate. Mere development such as 12 ♘d2 is not good enough to stop Black's kingside plan (12...♖g6! 13 ♔h1? ♘f4).

White tried **12 ♕h5**. Natural moves followed, **12...♘b4 13 ♘a3 ♖g6 14 ♗f4 b6**.

White to move

Black is ready to add pressure to g2 with ...♗b7.

If White blocks the g-file with 15 ♗g3, Black replies 15...♗d6.

Then 16 ♗xd6 cxd6! and 17...♖g5 would drive back White's queen (18 ♕h4? ♖xg2+ or 18 ♕f3 ♗d7 and ...♗c6).

White tried **15 ♕f3** and then **15...♗e6! 16 ♗xe6 fxe6 17 ♕e4**.

But the pressure on his weakest point increased after **17...♗d6 18 ♗xd6 cxd6!**, in view of ...♕g5 and ...d5.

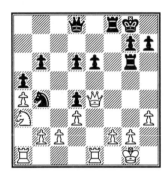

White to move

Black's kingside was collapsing after **19 ♕xd4 ♕g5 20 g3 ♕f5! 21 g4 h5!**.

Little of this could be foretold ten moves ago. But you don't need to calculate anywhere close to this position to choose 11...♖g6!. You need to see how g2 was weak and what it takes to exploit it.

Black won after **22 ♖e4 d5 23 ♔h2 ♕f3 24 ♖ee1 hxg4**.

Targets

Most games, like that one, really begin after move 10. This is when you have exhausted your opening knowledge and have to start thinking on your own.

It is when you should start thinking of targets, the most vulnerable pawns and pieces in your opponent's camp. They may provide your first plan. Identifying a target is often more important than completing development.

Take the King's Indian Defense (**1 d4 ♘f6 2 c4 g6 3 ♘f3 ♗g7**) as an example.

It once faced a critical test in the Fianchetto Variation (**4 g3 0-0 5 ♗g2 d6 6 0-0 ♘bd7 7 ♘c3 e5**) and its main line (**8 e4 exd4 9 ♘xd4 ♖e8**).

Even strong masters distrusted Black's cramped position.

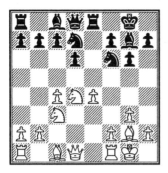

White to move

Black can complete development, such as with ...♘c5, ...♗d7, ...c6,...♛c7 and ...♖ad8. But he runs out of constructive moves while White chooses one of many strong middlegame plans.

What turned the King's Indian into a dreaded weapon was a new way of thinking: Black doesn't need ...♗d7 and ...♖ad8 to create counterplay. He needs good tactics and good targets.

An example of tactics is 10 ♗e3 ♘c5 11 ♛c2 ♘g4! and ...♘xe3.

White can rule out...♘g4 and remove the d4-knight from danger with **10 ♘4e2 ♘c5 11 f3**.

But then targets matter, after **11...♘fd7!**.

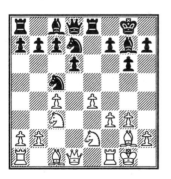

White to move

Black points out White's weakest point is the pawn at c4. The d7-knight can threaten it from e5 or b6.

If White stops ...♘e5 with 12 f4? he finds himself in trouble after 12...♘b6!.

For instance, 13 b3 ♗g4, with a threat of 14...♗xe2/...♗xc3. Then 14 ♗b2? ♘xe4! or 14 ♗d2 f5!.

Another revelation about targets arises if White tries **8 ♕c2**, instead of 8 e4.

In this way he ensures an e4-pawn will not be threatened. After **8...exd4 9 ♘xd4**:

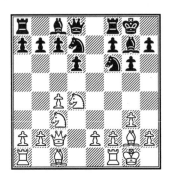

Black to move

This looks promising for White, in light of 9...♖e8 10 ♖d1!.

Then 10...♘b6? or 10...♘e5 invite 11 c5!. White will be the one exploiting a weakest point, Black's pawn at d6.

But suppose we replace the principled 9...♖e8 with the immediate **9...♘b6!**.

Then the threat of ...♘xc4 stops White from completing development. For example, 10 b3? c5! favors Black after 11 ♘f3 ♗f5 12 ♕d1 d5!. Or after 11 ♘db5 a6 12 ♘a3 ♗f5.

The difference between passive inferiority and Black counterplay is finding the right targets.

Squaring Off

Once you have identified a target, you naturally want to capture it. But the weakest point can be something you cannot capture – a square.

A square may be the most vulnerable point because your opponent will use his pieces to defend material, rather than squares. Yet that square can also be the most valuable target:

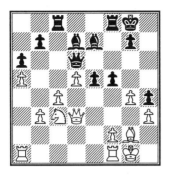

Caruana – Vachier-Lagrave
Wijk aan Zee 2015
Black to move

At first glance, the g4-pawn looks like White's weakest point. After 21...fxg4, Black wins it and corrupts White's kingside.

But White would have excellent survival chances after 22 ♔h1 followed by ♘e4 and ♖g1.

Black detected a much more valuable target – at h2.

He played **21...e4!** with the surprisingly strong idea of delivering mate via ...♗d8-c7! and ...♕h2.

For example, 22 ♕d4 ♕h6 would threaten to win a piece with 23...♗f6. Then 23 ♖ac1 ♗f6 24 ♕d1 ♗e5! and ...♕f4!.

White tried to foil that with **22 ♕e3**.

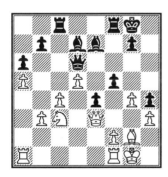

Black to move

But there was no good answer to **22...♗d8!**.

The h2-square is easily overlooked in the previous diagram. But now we can see that only the White king can defend it.

Black would win after 23 f4 exf3 24 ♖xf3 ♗c7 and ...♕h2+/...fxg4.

If, instead, the White king flees with 23 &fdl &c7 24 &fl, the compromised kingside is fatally pieced by 24... fxg4 25 &xe4 &h2, for example.

White saved his king by going into a bad endgame, **23 &xe4 fxe4 24 &xe4 &f4 25 &xf4**, but eventually lost.

While You Wait

The best time to think about the near future is after you have just made a move. While you wait for your opponent to reply, you can scan the board for a target. If the enemy king has few defending pieces, as in the last example, it is usually target No. 1. If the king is safe, his weakest point may be a vulnerable piece or a pawn.

Figuring out what that point is may be much harder than it appears.

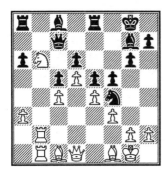

Boleslavsky – Kasparian
Moscow 1952
Black to move

White has just played 26 &b6. While he waits for Black to choose between 26...&b8 and 26...&a7, he can try to calculate his next move.

But he can use this time more usefully by asking himself to identify the weakest Black point.

Logically, it should be on the queenside, such as at b7 or b6. White's rooks can penetrate there after 26...&a7 27 &xc8 and &b6, followed by &c6.

But logic can lead us in another direction: Regardless of what Black does with his rook next move, White will need to play &xc8 eventually. Otherwise, the knight gets in the way of his doubled rooks.

Logic takes us one step further: Once White plays &xc8, what will the weakest point be?

As unlikely as it may seem, the answer is f5. For example, 26...♖b8 27 g3! ♘h5 28 ♗h3 can be followed by ♘xc8 and exf5!.

Play went **26...♖a7 27 g3! ♘h5 28 ♗h3**.

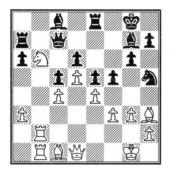

Black to move

The key square is doomed: 28...♖f8 29 ♕c2 ♗d7 allows 30 ♘xd7 ♕xd7 31 ♖b8 and wins.

Black conceded it with **28...♗d7 29 ♘xd7 ♕xd7 30 ♖b8 ♗f8 31 exf5** and White delivered a neat finish, **31...♖xb8 32 ♖xb8 gxf5 33 ♗h6 ♘g7 34 ♕b1 e4 35 fxe4 ♕f7 36 ♗xf5 ♕f6 37 e5! dxe5 38 ♗xh7+ ♔h8 39 ♗g5 resigns**.

Change of Theater

When your opponent has weaknesses on both wings, or one wing and the center, you may have a choice of middlegame targets. Your decision should be based on which is easier to attack. But that can change.

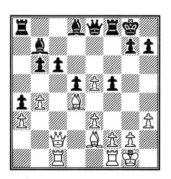

Simagin – Novotelnov
Moscow 1951
White to move

Black's last move was 20...♗b7, preventing ♕xc6. Given time, he can improve his chances with ...♕e6 followed by ...b5 and ...♗e7.

This indicates White needs a vigorous plan. He can find one by asking, "What is wrong with Black's last move?"

He would get the same answer if he asks, "What is the weakest point?"

The answer to the first question is that ...♗b7 made the f5-pawn vulnerable.

Can it be attacked? Yes, by ♗d3 – but also with g2-g4!.

White began his plan with **21 f4** and play continued **21...♗c7 22 ♗d3!**.

Black to move

It doesn't look like much has happened since ...♗b7. But Black is strategically lost because of the f5-square.

He can protect it with 22...g6 23 g4 ♕e6. But this allows the opening of the g-file.

He would be quickly outgunned on the kingside after 24 gxf5 gxf5 25 ♔h2! and ♖g1+ followed by ♖g5.

For example, 25...♔h8 26 ♖g1 ♖f7 27 ♖g5 ♖af8 28 ♖cg1 and ♕g2.

Black's other basic option is to abandon the defense of f5, after **22...♕e6 23 g4!**.

Black to move

But **23...fxg4** was only a temporary respite in view of **24 ♗xh7+ ♔h8 25 ♗g6!**.

Black could not stop the strategic killer 26 f5!.

For example, 25...gxh3 26 f5! ♕e7 27 ♖f3 and ♖xh3+.

The rest was increasing desperation – **25...c5 26 f5! ♕e7 27 hxg4 ♕h4 28 ♖f2 ♔g8 29 ♖h2 ♕xg4+ 30 ♖g2 ♕h3 31 bxc5 ♗xe5 32 ♕e2 ♗xd4 33 exd4 ♖f6 34 ♕e7 bxc5 35 ♗h5 resigns**.

Arithmetic

White recognized in that game that his queenside pressure had reached a dead end after 20...♗b7. But how did he guess he had good chances of success of attacking f5? Arithmetic helped. Here's another illustration.

Mokry – Lanc
Trnava 1988
White to move

Black has just played 17...♕d7. He would be nearly equal after 18 ♗c2 ♗f5! and only slightly worse after 18 ♘xe6 ♕xe6.

White exploited his opponent's last move with **18 ♗a4!**. Then 18...♕c8? 19 ♗xe7 or 18...♕b7 19 ♘xe6 fxe6 20 ♕g4 would clearly favor him.

Play went **18...b5**, and now **19 ♘xe6! fxe6 20 ♗c2** created a position worth assessing.

Who has gained ground since the diagram?

"White has," a student might say. "Because Black has doubled pawns."

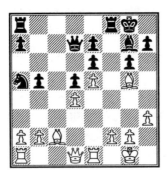

Black to move

He is half right. White's advantage has grown considerably and ...fxe6 is the reason.

But the Black e-pawns are not the weakest Black points. They cannot be easily attacked.

The best target is the Black kingside, and we can ask Mikhail Tal why. Tal used arithmetic to gauge whether a wing attack would succeed:

Count the number of potential attacking pieces. Then count the number of defenders.

If the ratio is 1-to-1, chances of success are iffy. If you add more attackers, the chances increase. The greater the numerical ratio favors the attacker, the greater the likelihood of success, Tal said.

He was talking about attacking a wing. But we want to know about a specific square, the weakest point.

Here this means g6. This became clearer after **20...♖ac8 21 ♖c1 ♘c6 22 ♗b1 ♖c7 23 h4!.**

Black to move

A mismatch is looming on g6. White will attack it with h4-h5 and then with heavy pieces, such as his queen on g4 and a rook on g3.

Black's queen and king are the only potential protectors of g6. This is not enough (23...♕e8 24 ♖c3 h5 25 ♖g3).

If Black meets h4-h5 with ...g6xh5, a new target is exposed at h7, and its ratio of potential attackers and defenders is also lopsided.

The game went **23...♘d8 24 h5 ♘f7 25 ♖xc7 ♕xc7 26 ♗e3**.

Black to move

The trend is getting easier to detect. We can see how futile 26...g5 27 ♕d3 and 26...gxh5 27 ♕xh5 h6 28 ♕g6 are.

The rest was **26...♘h6 27 hxg6 ♘f5 28 ♕h5 h6 29 ♗xf5 ♖xf5 30 ♕h3 ♕c2 31 ♖c1 ♕e2 32 ♖c8+ ♗f8 33 g7 resigns**.

In retrospect, the outcome after 23 h4 was a matter of three being greater than two. Three potential attacking pieces against a king and (maybe) a defending queen.

Higher Mathematics

The ratio of attacking pieces to protecting pieces is not always clear. Pieces on the queenside might suddenly join a kingside assault. Then, even a world champion can find himself struggling to defend.

Botvinnik – Simagin, Moscow 1951

1 d4 d5 2 c4 e6 3 ♘c3 c6 4 e3 ♘f6 5 ♘f3 ♘bd7 6 ♗d3 dxc4 7 ♗xc4 b5 8 ♗d3 a6 9 e4 c5 10 e5 cxd4 11 ♘xb5 axb5 12 exf6 ♗b7 13 0-0 gxf6 14 ♗xb5 ♖g8

127

Individually, each of Black's last three moves could be played without a plan in mind. Together, they take aim at g2 and f3.

White to move

But hold on. How can g2 be considered weak? Only Black's g8-rook seems able to threaten it.

In addition, White can defend g2 with the help of another piece. One way is ♖e1 and ♗f1. Another way is blocking the g-file with ♗f4-g3.

However, the arithmetic can change. Black may add his a8-rook to the mix with ...♖a5!. Then, if the b5-bishop retreats, ...♘e5! would exert powerful pressure on f3.

Computers initially see a big White advantage after 15 g3 but then shrink the evaluation as they crunch variations.

For example, 15...♖a5 16 a4 ♖xb5! 17 axb5 ♘e5 Black would be winning after 18 ♘xe5 ♖xg2+ or 18 ♘e1 ♗b4 and ...♗xe1.

Instead, play continued **15 ♗f4 ♖a5!**.

White to move

Black's idea was 16 ♕e2? ♖xb5 17 ♕xb5 ♗xf3.

On 16 ♗e2? ♘e5!, he threatens to win with 17...d3.

For instance, 17 ♘e1 d3 18 ♗f3 ♘xf3+ 19 ♘xf3 ♕d5!.

Since ...♘e5 is a danger, World Champion Mikhail Botvinnik might have eliminated the knight with 16 ♗xd7+ and blocked the g-file with 17 ♗g3.

But Black would have the better winning chances due to his two-bishop advantage and a solid center after 17...e5 and ...♕d5.

The best defense was also the most principled move, **16 a4!**.

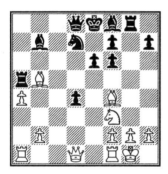

Black to move

Now 16...e5 17 ♗g3 would allow White to say the weakest points on the board are on Black's side.

One of those is f5, which White might exploit with ♘h4-f5.

Another is h7, which he can try to exploit with ♘h4 and ♕h5.

Black realized this was a pivotal moment of the game. His situation is urgent and that called for **16...♖xb5! 17 axb5 ♘e5**.

White to move

Black threatened a winning capture on f3. Clearly 18 ♘xe5?? ♖xg2+ is taboo.

White can avert disaster with 18 ♗g3 or 18 ♘e1 and be the Exchange ahead. But in either case Black would have ample compensation.

For example, 18 ♗g3 ♘xf3+ 19 gxf3 ♕d5. Black might grab the b5- or f3-pawn but his most dangerous idea is ...h5-h4.

Also good for him is 18 ♘e1 ♗c5 and 18...♕d5 19 f3 ♗d6.

Botvinnik decided he had to give the Exchange back with ♖a7xb7. He chose **18 ♗xe5 fxe5 19 ♖a7**, and a fighting draw followed **19...♕d5 20 ♖xb7 ♕xb7 21 g3**.

Weak, Weaker, Weakest

As you improve, it will become easier to identify a weak point. What remains difficult is determining whether it is the weakest point.

You can arrive at the right answer in different ways. But you can be misled about the weakest of the weak.

Anand – Kasparov
Moscow 1995
White to move

If arithmetic could talk, it would tell us: "This is a no-brainer. Black is weakest at d6. White has more heavy pieces to attack it than Black has to defend it."

But when you begin calculating, it isn't that simple. The immediate 21 ♖xd6? liquidates winning chances (21...♖xd6 22 ♖xd6 ♘xa2).

All right, suppose we forget about our friend arithmetic. If we search for weak squares we can get another answer: "Black is weakest on the queenside because of b6."

That can be exploited by 21 ♘a4! and 22 ♕b6. A trade of queens would doom the d-pawn.

If Black replies 21...b5, then 22 cxb5 axb5 23 ♘c3 is trouble (23...♖dc8 24 ♘xb5 ♘xa2 25 ♘xd6).

Not bad. But there is a third answer to the checklist question: "Black is weakest on the kingside. Only his king defends it."

White opted for **21 h4!**.

Black to move

He prepared 22 h5 followed by 23 f4.

His queen will be almost unopposed on the kingside after, for example, 23 f4 ♘ec6 24 ♕h3 and then ♕h4-f6 with the idea of h5-h6 and mate on g7.

Computers find Black losing after 21...♘ec6 22 h5 ♘e7 23 h6, with a last-rank mating threat after 24 c5!.

No better is 21...h5, because of 22 f4 ♘g4 23 ♗xg4 hxg4 24 f5. Or 22...♘ec6 23 ♕g3 with f4-f5 to some.

The position was suddenly desperate for Garry Kasparov. He diverted White's attention with **21...b5 22 cxb5 axb5**.

White to move

Kasparov appeared to have counterplay (23 ♗xb5 ♘g4). But this was a mirage. He was lost after **23 ♘xb5! ♘bc6 24 a3**.

He resigned after **24...d5 25 exd5 ♖xd5 26 ♖xd5 exd5 27 b4 ♕a4 28 ♖xd5**.

Neighborhood Effect

I hear some readers protesting: "The real reason White attacked the kingside in that game is that a king is a more valuable target than a weak pawn or square."

But if you always follow that logic you will find yourself throwing your pieces at an impregnable king position.

The best target is the most vulnerable one. Even if is just a square, seizing control of it can open neighboring squares to invasion. Then the whole sector can collapse. Here's how this happens.

Geller – Simagin, Moscow 1951

1 d4 d5 2 c4 e6 3 ♘c3 ♘f6 4 ♘f3 c5 5 cxd5 ♘xd5 6 e3 ♗e7 7 ♗d3 ♘xc3 8 bxc3 ♘d7 9 0-0 0-0 10 e4 b6 11 ♗f4 ♗b7 12 ♕e2 g6 13 ♖fd1 cxd4 14 cxd4 ♗f6

White to move

The exchange of c-pawns helped Black in two ways. It made the d4-pawn a potential target and it gave him a good way to develop his a8-rook, on c8.

But was there a drawback to 13...cxd4? Yes, a subtle one.

By opening the c-file, it turned c7 into a potential invasion square for a White rook.

This made **15 ♖ac1!** stand out.

Black would be paralyzed after 16 ♖c7! ♗c8 17 ♕c2 or 16...♖b8 17 ♗b5!.

He naturally parried the ♖c7 threat with **15...♖c8**.

He was one move (16...♕e7) away from being able to play a competitive middlegame.

White to move

White could win control of the open file with 16 ♖xc8! ♕xc8 17 ♖c1. He would have a serious edge after 17...♕a8 18 ♗b5 or 18 ♖c7.

But he noticed the weakness of squares in the neighborhood of c7, namely b7 and a6.

To exploit them, he needed to trade bishops quickly. If he allowed 16...♕e7 then 17 ♗a6 ♘b8! would be harmless.

After **16 ♗a6** Black was virtually forced into **16...♗xa6 17 ♕xa6**.

The weakness of b7 seemed remote in the diagram but would be real after 17...♖a8 18 ♕b7!.

This is why Black protected b7 and the a7-pawn with **17...♖xc1 18 ♖xc1 ♕a8**.

That also deterred 19 ♖c7 in view of 19...♕xe4!.

White to move

133

White can avert …♕xe4 by means of **19 e5** (19…♗g7 20 ♖c7).

But there is a complicating trick: 19…♕b8! covers c7.

The right way to make the c7-square matter was **19 ♗d6!**.

Then 19…♖e8 20 e5 would allow White to dominate the c-file (20…♗d8 21 ♖c8, 20…♗e7 21 ♗xe7 ♖xe7 22 ♖c8+ or 20…♗g7 21 ♖c7 and wins).

Black resigned shortly after **19…♖d8 20 e5 ♗g7 21 ♖c7! ♕e4 22 ♘d2** (also 22 ♗e7) **♕e1+ 23 ♘f1**.

A cute finish would have been 23…♘b8 24 ♕c8! ♖xc8 25 ♖xc8+ ♗f8 26 ♗xf8 and wins.

Flip

When you find yourself having to defend, the checklist question can be turned around. You can ask yourself, "What is *my* weakest point?"

This is more difficult than it seems because you can't easily see what you opponent sees. You are sitting in the wrong chair to do this.

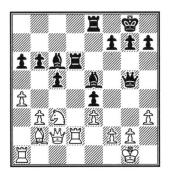

Cori – Pichot
Internet 2020
White to move

If you play over this game from White's perspective, the position may seem easily defendable by White. But if you look at it from Black's viewpoint, the picture is quite different: Black has a juicy target at g2.

If White had seen that he would have safeguarded his kingside with ♘e2 earlier. Even now 25 ♖xd6 and ♘e2 held out hope.

But **25 ♖ad1??** left g2 defenseless following **25…♖g6!**.

He resigned soon after **26 g3 ♗xg3! 27 fxg3 ♕xe3+ 28 ♔f1 ♕xg3** and …e3.

Little better was 26 g4 ♖h6 26 ♔g2 ♕f6 and …♕f3+.

Another reason defending is difficult is you can make matters worse by protecting the right sector of the board but the wrong squares.

Kasparov – Short
Zürich 2001
Black to move

Nigel Short understood his kingside was a potential target and realized his opponent was recruiting an assault army. He guessed that h7 was his weakest point and played **16…♘df8.**

What is the upside to this move? Answer: h7 is well guarded.

What is the downside? Answer: g7 is more vulnerable.

Short's move made it weaker because he cannot safeguard it with …♗f8!.

White to move

This was enough reason for Garry Kasparov to start calculating sacrifices in the neighborhood of g7.

But 17 ♗h6? gxh6 18 ♕d2 is too slow. Black would have time to repair the damage of his 16th move with 18…♘d7 and 19…♗f8!.

More promising is 17 ♘xg7 ♔xg7 18 h5. White would win after 18…♘h8? 19 ♘h2 and ♕g4+.

135

However, 18...♘d7 19 ♕d2 ♖h8 20 ♕h6+ ♔g8 was not easy to calculate to a clear conclusion.

Kasparov chose the useful **17 ♔g2**. It made ♘xg7 stronger because h4-h5 and ♖h1 would be available.

Black to move

Black still had time to undo 16...♘df8? with 17...♘d7! and ...♗f8.

But he sought queenside play with **17...♕d7** and ...♕xb5. For instance, 18 ♕e2? cxd4 19 cxd4 ♖ac8.

Kasparov alertly saw 17...♕d7?? was a blunder because it made g7 indefensible: The ...♘d7/...♗f8 resource had been fatally delayed.

He could have tried to calculate 18 ♘xg7 to a conclusion. But he didn't need to – because **18 ♗h6!** won quickly.

The game ended soon after 18...gxh6 19 ♕d2 (threat of ♕xh6-g7 mate) f5 20 exf6 ♗d8 21 ♕xh6 and ♘g5.

Let's go back to the first diagram. Short was right to defend his kingside. But a closer look shows that White cannot easily attack h7 because his h5-knight gets in the way of ♕h5 as well as of h4-h5.

Black should have kept his options open (...♗f8 or ...♘df8) and sought queenside counterplay with 16...cxd4! 17 cxd4 ♕c7 and ...♖ac8. His chances would be at least equal to White's.

Bernstein's Irony

When you have identified your own weakest point and gotten a sense of your defensive options, there is another question to consider: Is it worth defending?

It makes sense to ask because you would not otherwise realize the cost of defense.

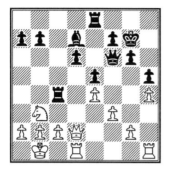

Leko – Carlsen
Miskolc 2008
Black to move

If we rank the weakest points on the board, No. 1 is the d6-pawn. A distant second is the c2-pawn. It is more easily defended.

This position had arisen in previous games. Black had unpleasant experiences protecting his pawn, with 19...♖c6 20 ♕a5 and 19...♖e6 20 ♕e3.

But **19...♖ec8!** changed the evaluation of the position dramatically.

Black's weakness was gone, along with a pawn, after **20 ♕xd6 ♗e6**.

White to move

Ossip Bernstein, a great but forgotten 20th century player, made an ironic observation: When you give up a weak pawn, your position seems to improve. The reason is that some of your pieces are freed from defensive duties and can be reassigned to offense.

This improvement may be an illusion: Your new freedom of movement is temporary and the chief benefit of abandoning the weakness is psychological. You feel better being the aggressor.

But Bernstein's observation often succeeds and it does here. With the d6-pawn off the board, the c2-pawn is the main topic of conversation. It is underprotected: White would be slightly worse after 21 ♕d3 ♖xc2 22 ♕xc2 ♖xc2 23 ♔xc2 in view of 23...a5! and ...a4.

Worse is 21 ♖d2? ♖xc2 22 ♖xc2 ♖xc2 (23 ♔xc2?? ♗xb3+).

After **21 c3 b5** Black can find other queenside targets. For example, 22...♖4c6 23 ♕d2 b4! and 24 cxb4 ♗xb3 25 axb3 ♖b8 followed by ...♖cb6.

White sought to trade queens, with **22 ♕d2 a5 23 ♕g5**. He agreed to a draw soon after **23...♕xg5 24 hxg5 a4 25 ♘d2 ♖4c7**.

What To Remember

Good planning and good counterplay stem from finding targets for your pieces. The best target can be anything from the enemy king to a weak square. You can evaluate how vulnerable the target is by counting up the number of potential attacking pieces and comparing it with the number of potential defenders. You should also be aware of your own weakest points. And you should be willing to abandon their defense when it is too burdensome.

Quiz

58.

Komarov – Razuvaev
Reggio Emilia 1996-7
White to move

Which is Black's weakest point? How can White target it?

59.

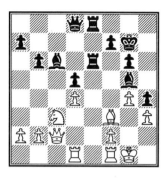

Beliavsky – Kramnik
Belgrade 1997
Black to move

The weakest point on the board is not the Black d5-pawn. What is?

60.

Morovic – Karpov
Dos Hermanas 1994
Black to move

What is Black's best source of counterplay?

61.

Timman – Smyslov
Bugojno 1984
White to move

How does White exploit Black's weaknesses?

62.

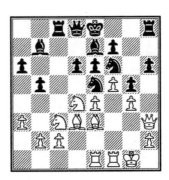

Milos – J. Polgar
Sao Paolo 1996
Black to move

Which pieces are Black's targets and how can she reach them?

63.

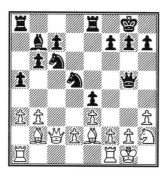

Caruana – Karjakin
Stavanger 2018
White to move

Both sides have potential targets. What should White do?

64.

Short – Hjartarson
Amsterdam 1991
White to move

Black has potential weaknesses at a5, d6 and f6. Which is weakest?

65.

Gulko – Ehlvest
Horgen 1995
Black to move

There is an arithmetic imbalance coming. Where?

66.

Campora – Dreev
Moscow 1989
Black to move

How should Black proceed?

67.

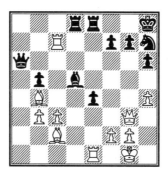

Kashdan – Reshevsky
Hollywood 1945
White to move

White lost after **35 ♔h2 ♘f6**. What did he miss?

68.

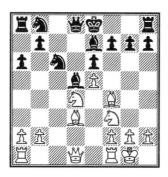

Inarkiev – Ryazantsev
Olginka 2011
Black to move

Black has easy equality with 13...♘xd4 14 ♘xd4 ♘c6. What is better?

69.

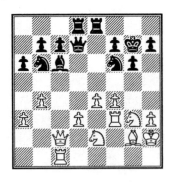

Smyslov – Suetin
Moscow 1952
White to move

To find White's best move you can also ask, "What is the best tactical idea?"

70. Tari – Caruana, Stavanger 2020

1 e4 c5 2 ♘f3 e6 3 d4 cxd4 4 ♘xd4 ♘c6 5 ♘c3 ♕c7 6 g3 a6 7 ♗g2 ♘f6 8 0-0 ♘xd4 9 ♕xd4 ♗c5 10 ♗f4 d6 11 ♕d2 h6 12 ♖ad1 e5 13 ♗e3 ♗xe3 14 fxe3

Black to move

Evaluate the position.

Chapter Six:
What Does He Want?

After one of his great kingside attacks, Bobby Fischer said the most difficult move of the game for him to find was a2-a3. It was an innocuous, seemingly irrelevant move on the side of the board opposite his attack.

But it stopped his opponent's counterplay and granted him a free hand to win on the kingside. "Chess is a matter of delicate judgment, knowing when to punch and when to duck," Fischer explained.

Knowing when to take a precaution like this is essentially a matter of figuring out what your opponent would like to do.

Haba – Lechtýnský
Karlovy Vary 2005
White to move

White can sense he is close to a forced win. He has two promising ideas that might end resistance.

One is a seventh-rank pin with 26 ♖a7. This threatens to win the underprotected knight with 27 ♖d1!.

But 26...♕d6 is an adequate defense. Black remains alive after 27 ♕g4? ♘c5, for example.

The second tactical idea is a capture on f6, followed by ♕xg7 mate. This needs the support of **26 ♖f1!**.

Black's best try was **26...♖b8**.

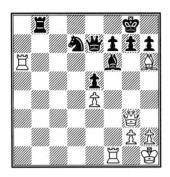

White to move

White saw the point: Now 27 ♖axf6? is punished by 27...♕xf6!.

White can lose after 28 ♖xf6?? ♖b1+ and mates.

After 26...♖b8, a computer would calculate White's many options and discover that he has a forced win. For humans, there is an easier way.

White should look at the board from Black's point of view. Then White would see that ...♖b1+ is not only Black's best idea but also his only real chance to save himself.

This led to **27 h3!**. It only does one thing. It provides an escape square for White's king in case of ...♖b1+.

But this is enough. Black would be lost after 27...g6 28 ♖a7!.

He resigned after **27...♘b6 28 ♕g4** (or 28 ♗e3 ♘d7 29 ♕g4 and ♖a7) **♕d6 29 ♖xf6!**. Also lost was 28...♕e6 27 ♕xe6 fxe6 28 ♖b1.

Ounce Of Prevention

Masters call moves like 27 h3 "prophylactic," a term usually used to mean preventing disease. In chess it means anticipating danger.

Prophylactic moves are easy to misunderstand. Beginners quickly learn their value. Then they play them too much.

As White, they don't like it when a Black bishop pins their f3-knight with ...♗g4. So they spend a tempo on h2-h3. In most cases, this is a wasted move and often an unnecessary weakening.

Timing makes a big difference, as Fischer said. For example, the old main line of the Ruy Lopez runs **1 e4 e5 2 ♘f3 ♘c6 3 ♗b5 a6 4 ♗a4 ♘f6 5 0-0 ♗e7 6 ♖e1 b5 7 ♗b3 0-0 8 c3 d6**.

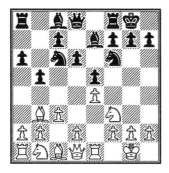

White to move

After **9 d4 ♗g4!** Black readies 10...♗xf3 so that 11 ♕xf3 exd4 wins a pawn.

The pinning 9...♗g4 usually leads to a double-edged change in the center, e.g. 10 d5 ♘a5 11 ♗c2 c6!.

However, ...♗g4 is Black's best source of counterplay. Once it is stopped, by **9 h3!**, White should enjoy a small but lasting advantage, as countless games have shown.

Prophylaxis doesn't sound like a real skill because it is essentially negative. When Garry Kasparov played his first match against a computer, he won. One of the defeated programmers said ruefully that it "didn't get a chance to show what it can do."

Kasparov was happy to hear that. "That's exactly the point!" he said. "The highest art of a chess player lies in not allowing the opponent to show what he can do."

Mind Reading

The easiest way to determine if you should play a prophylactic move is to ask yourself, "What does he want?"

Petrosian – Ivkov
Nice 1974
White to move

147

Nothing much is happening, according to the checklist questions we've considered so far. But Tigran Petrosian looked ahead by looking backward:

Black's last move was ...♖ae8. What was his idea?

It was a principled, developing move. But Petrosian realized it can also be part of a plan to seize the initiative, with ...♖e7,...♖fe8 and ...e4! followed by ...e3!.

This would take at least four moves. But Petrosian liked to smother ideas like this even before they occurred to his opponent.

He chose **19 f3!**.

Black to move

Black understood ...e4 was off the table now. But, like Petrosian, he looked for another reason for his opponent's last move. What did *White* want?

One answer is 19 f3 created the option of g2-g4. Then Black's f5-knight would have no promising retreat. Depending on the situation, ...♘e7 might allow a strong ♘e6.

Of course, White may have had no intention to play g2-g4. But just in case, Black replied **19...♘g7**, so e6 was well guarded.

White to move

Then it was Petrosian's turn to try to read his opponent's mind. Black had anticipated 20 g4. But was there another reason he played 19...♞g7 ?

Petrosian found an answer: Black's cramped position would be eased by a trade of bishops, after 20...♗f5!. Petrosian stopped this with **20 g4!**.

This appears to weaken the kingside. But Black felt he had no real prospects for counterchances there. He looked for queenside play, such as with ...b5.

This push would take preparation, because the immediate 20...b5? 21 cxb5 ♗xb5? loses to 22 c4!.

If Black signals his intent with 20...a6, Petrosian would likely reply with another prophylactic move, 21 a4!. Black anticipated this anticipation with **20...♛a4!**.

White to move

Black would finally have counterplay if 21 ♛b2 ♖b8 and 22...b5 happens.

Petrosian could head this off by entering a favorable endgame, 21 ♛xa4 and 22 ♖ab1.

But he chose **21 ♛b3** because 21...♛xb3 22 axb3 is a better endgame. He would have his choice of a queenside plan (b3-b4 and ♖fb1) or a kingside plan (h2-h3 and f3-f4!).

Black should have tried 21...♛a6, with the idea of 22...♞xd5! 22 cxd5 ♛xd3.

But the game continued **21...♖b8 22 ♗c2 ♛a5**.

This gave Petrosian one more chance for prophylaxis, **23 a4!**.

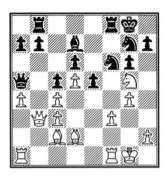

Black to move

Computers may conclude White's advantage has not grown since 19 f3.

But the cumulative effect of 19 f3!, 20 g4! and 23 a4! wiped out Black's chances for counterplay.

White's superiority became clearer following **23... ♕c7 24 h3 a6 25 a5 b5 26 axb6!** (not 26 cxb5? ♖xb5 27 ♕a3 c4!) **♖xb6 27 ♕a3** and he won soon after **27...♕d8 28 ♕c1 ♕e7 29 ♕e1 ♖b2 30 ♗d3 ♗c8 31 ♗c1 ♖b3 32 ♗c2 ♖b6 33 f4! h6 34 fxe5 ♕xe5 35 ♕xe5 dxe5 36 ♘e4** and **♗a3!**.

Prophylaxis Power

Petrosian made so many quiet, unassuming moves in his career, it was difficult to realize they were powerfully prophylactic until after his opponent resigned.

Petrosian – Larsen, Beverwijk 1960

1 c4 d6 2 d4 e5 3 ♘f3 ♘d7 4 ♘c3 ♘gf6 5 e4 ♗e7 6 ♗e2 0-0 7 0-0 c6 8 d5 ♘c5 9 ♘d2 a5

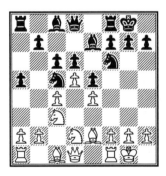

White to move

150

Bent Larsen's last move stopped b2-b4. But it was not just defensive. He intended 10...cxd5!, followed by ...a4.

After 11 cxd5 a4!, Larsen would be at least equal and could easily get the upper hand after ...&d7 and ...b5. The same goes for 11 exd5 a4 and ...♕b6.

Petrosian's **10 b3!** looked overly cautious. But he had discouraged ...a4 because of the favorable reply b3-b4!.

The game proceeded with **10...cxd5 11 cxd5 &d7.**

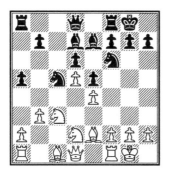

White to move

Larsen was not done. He had another queenside idea, 12...b5!.

It is based on short tactics (13 &xb5 ♘fxe4! 14 ♘dxe4 ♘xe4 15 ♘xe4 &xb5).

Petrosian could have stopped this by protecting his e4-pawn with 12 ♖e1.

But **12 a4!** was superior because it prepared a desirable trade of Black's good bishop (&b5).

Larsen began to realize he was being outplayed after **12...♕b6 13 &a3 ♖fc8 14 ♖b1 ♕a7 15 ♖c1 ♖c7 16 &b5!.**

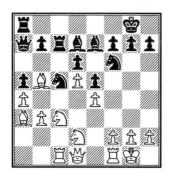

Black to move

If the light-squared bishops are traded, Petrosian could plant a knight on b5 or c4, or both, with a major strategic edge.

Larsen avoided this with **16...♗g4** and allowed his bishop to be marginalized by **17 ♕e1 ♘a6 18 h3! ♗h5**.

Larsen regarded Petrosian as his "twin" because they were both disciples of Aron Nimzovich. Here Larsen was poised to create a Nimzovichian blockade of the queenside with ...♘b4! and ...♘d7-c5!.

But his twin knew what Larsen wanted. After **19 ♗xa6! ♕xa6 20 ♘c4**, Petrosian was ready to deliver a positional coup de grace with ♘b5. That could be followed by a capture on d6 or e5.

Larsen thwarted this with a desperate sacrifice of the Exchange, **20...♖xc4 21 bxc4 ♕xc4**, and was ground down.

Where did he begin to lose the game? Was it when he allowed 12 a4? Or when Petrosian played 16 ♗b5?

No, this below-the-radar battle turned against Black after **10...cxd5?**.

The more accurate **10...♗d7!** would have retained pawn control of b5 and enabled him to develop smoothly, after 11 a4, with...♕b6 and ...♖ac8, or with ...♘fd7 and ...♗g5 and a trade of bishops.

Ugly

Prophylactic moves can be hard to appreciate because they are quiet, like 10 b3! and 12 a4! in that game. They can look ugly because they contradict general principles.

They are not inherently anti-principle. They are *anti-counterplay*. They should be judged primarily by what they stop.

Keres – Flohr, Semmering-Baden 1937

1 d4 ♘f6 2 c4 g6 3 ♘f3 ♗g7 4 g3 c6 5 ♗g2 d5 6 cxd5 ♘xd5 7 0-0 0-0 8 ♘c3 ♘xc3 9 bxc3 c5 10 ♗a3 cxd4

White to move

152

The principled recapture is, of course, 11 cxd4. How could there be a drawback?

The answer is that 11 cxd4 would give Black a target at d4 to attack with 11...♘c6!.

He would stand well after 12 e3 ♕a5 13 ♗b2 ♗e6, for example.

In contrast, **11 ♘xd4!** left White with a glaring weakness, the isolated pawn at c3.

But a visible weakness is not a real weakness unless it can be attacked.

Black to move

Black lacks the development to exploit the c3-pawn. The d4-knight prevents him from developing smoothly.

For example, 11...♘c6? 12 ♘xc6 bxc6 runs into 13 ♕xd8 ♖xd8 14 ♗xe7 (14...♖e8? 15 ♗xc6).

Or 14...♖d2 15 ♖fd1 ♗xc3 16 ♖xd2 ♗xd2 17 ♖d1.

Black replied **11...♕c7**. It does three things:

It makes a threat, 12...♕xc3. It prepares ...♘c6 under safer conditions. And it is also prophylactic. White's best middlegame plan is to pound at b7. Black's move protected b7 before it is threatened.

White to move

Now 12 ♕d3 could be met by another prophylactic move, 12...a6!.

It stops ♘b5, which is a crucial tactic. For example, 12 ♕d3 ♘a6 13 ♖ab1 ♖d8 14 ♘b5!, with advantage to White.

Paul Keres chose **12 ♕b3**. Then 12...♘a6 13 ♖ab1 ♘c5 would turn out well following 14 ♕b4! (14...♘e6 15 ♘b5).

Black couldn't play 12...♘d7 13 ♗xe7!. But he missed his last chances for ...♘c6 here and on the next move.

Play went **12...♗f6 13 ♖fd1 ♘d7 14 c4** (14 ♖ac1!) **♘c5 15 ♕b4 ♘e6 16 ♘b5** and Keres won one of his greatest games, **16... ♕e5 17 ♖ac1 ♖d8 18 ♖d5! ♖xd5 19 cxd5 a6 20 ♘a7! ♘d4 21 ♖xc8+ ♖xc8 22 ♘xc8 ♕xe2 23 h4 ♘f5 24 ♕e4 resigns**.

Wider Net

Prophylaxis provides a new criterion for evaluating a candidate. This means you can cast a wider net when seeking the best move.

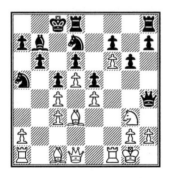

Fine – Beckhardt
New York 1933
White to move

Black threatens to get a good game with 16...♘xf6.

The natural defense of the f6-pawn is 16 ♕f3. But it has a drawback. The queen is also needed to defend the c4-pawn after 16...♗a6.

The unlikely solution to White's problem is **16 ♘h1!**. Then 16...♘xf6? 17 g3 wins a piece.

But the situation is much worse for Black than this indicates. White threatens to trap the queen with 17 g3! and 17...♕h3 18 ♘f2 ♕h5 19 ♗e2.

What Does He Want?

Black saved his queen with **16...♘f8**, so that 17 g3 ♛h3 18 ♘f2 ♛d7.

But he soon fell apart: **17 ♗e3 ♗a6 18 ♖b1 ♗xc4? 19 g3 ♛h3 20 ♗xc4 ♘xc4 21 ♛e2 ♘xe3 22 ♛a6+ ♔b8 23 ♖xb6+!**.

Black resigned in view of 23...axb6 24 ♛xb6+ ♔a8 25 ♛a6+.

Mysterious

Don't expect to find prophylactic moves easily. They are often puzzling because they don't have an obvious point.

When Aron Nimzovich put a rook on a closed file, it was called mysterious. But it made sense if you looked at the position from his opponent's side of the board.

Rubinstein – Nimzovich
Marienbad 1925
Black to move

Nimzovich didn't have to search for White's weakest points. The pawns at a2, a4 and c4 are all in his gun sights.

When he looks for the best move, he could start with 18...♖xa4.

But White could get back in the game with 19 a3 ♘c6 20 ♗xf6!.

The point is 20...exf6 21 ♛c2! would get his queen out of the d2-h6 pin and allow him to drop a knight onto d5.

An alternative to 18...♖xa4 is 18...♛a6. But again 19 a3 ♘c6 20 ♗xf6 improves White's chances (20... exf6 21 ♛xd6).

There was a lot to calculate but Nimzovich detected a repeating feature of these scenarios. White needed to play ♗xf6!.

This explains **18...♖fe8!**.

155

White to move

If you play over many Nimzovich games you will find moves that were very profound and others that were just a waste of time. This time: profound.

He had found a way to prepare 19...♖xa4 or 19...♕a6 without fear of ♗xf6. The e-file would become tactically toxic for White after ...exf6.

White could try 19 a3 ♘c6 20 ♖b1. But that creates a nasty pin on the b-file after 20...♖a6 and ...♖b6.

Akiba Rubinstein could not find anything better than **19 ♗xf6 exf6** and then **20 ♔f2**, to protect the e3-knight.

Black to move

What is wrong with White's last move? Nimzovich's reply, **20...f5!**, pointed it out.

His bishop will go to g7, where it threatens ...♗xa1 but would also exploit White's king's position with ...♗d4!.

There was no long-term defense, as 21 f4 ♗g7 22 ♖b1 ♕e4 and 21 a3 ♖xa4 indicate.

Rubinstein became desperate with **21 ♕xd6 ♗g7 22 ♖b1** and lost a piece after **22...♗d4!**.

He was ground down following **23 ♔g2 ♗xe3 24 ♘xe3 ♖xe3 25 ♕xc5 ♖xe2+ 26 ♖f2 ♖xf2+ 27 ♕xf2 ♖xa4**.

Crazy Killer

A bizarre-looking move can be justified by the tactical idea it employs. The reverse applies to a move that stifles a tactical idea: A prophylactic move that appears crazy can be a killer.

Gujrathi – Krasenkow, Wijk aan Zee 2018

1 e4 c5 2 ♘f3 e6 3 d4 cxd4 4 ♘xd4 ♘f6 5 ♘c3 ♘c6 6 ♘xc6 bxc6 7 e5 ♘d5 8 ♘e4 ♕c7 9 f4 ♕b6 10 c4 ♗b4+ 11 ♔e2

This move is easy to understand when you look at the alternatives (11 ♗d2? ♕e3+! and 11 ♘d2? ♘xf4).

Next came **11...f5 12 exf6 ♘xf6 13 ♗e3 ♕d8 14 ♘d6+ ♗xd6 15 ♕xd6 ♕e7 16 ♗c5 ♕f7**.

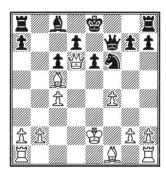

White to move

Why would Black prefer to stay in a bad middlegame rather than trade into a merely poor endgame with 16...♕xd6 ?

It's a good question and is another way of asking, "What does Black want?" The answer is 17...♘e4! is his best chance of survival.

For instance, 17 g3? ♘e4! 18 ♕e5 ♘xc5 19 ♕xc5 ♕f6.

White can stop the knight fork by moving his king to d3, e3 or f3. Each of the three moves looks weird but works.

White chose **17 ♔e3**.

Black to move

After the desperate **17...g5**, White could have safely played 18 fxg5.

Instead, he chose **18 ♗e2**. It also wins because of 18...gxf4+19 ♕xf4 and ♖af1.

Black was lost after **18...g4 19 ♖ac1 h5 20 ♖c3 ♕g7 21 ♗d3 ♔f7** and resigned after **22 ♔d2 ♖e8 23 ♖e1 ♕h6 24 ♔c2 a5 25 ♖e5 ♘h7 26 ♖f5+ ♔g8 27 ♕e5**.

Swindle Protection

"What does he want?" remains important as you close in on victory. Asking this is the best way to avoid being swindled.

Kashdan – Apšenieks
Folkestone 1933
White to move

White appears poised to win with 35 h4, followed by 36 ♕f4 and ♕g5 mate.

He would answer 35...♖c1, for example, with 36 ♕d6 mate.

But when you think you have a move that seems to end the game, it pays – more than ever – to put yourself in your opponent's shoes.

Here White saw Black was threatening his own mate, 35...♕xf1+! 36 ♔xf1 ♖c1+.

White found **35 ♔h2!**. Then 35...♕xf1 36 ♕e4+ mates. But the main point is it stops Black's only tactical idea, the queen sacrifice.

Black resigned after **35...♔f6 36 ♕d8+ ♔e6 37 ♖e7+ ♔f6 38 ♕f8+**.

What To Remember

Prophylactic moves don't punch. They duck. They are judged primarily by what they stop. This means you can consider a wider variety of moves than you normally might. This includes candidates that appear innocuous, ugly, mysterious, even crazy. But they can be as powerful as a strong tactical idea and are often the best way to avoid being swindled.

Quiz

71.

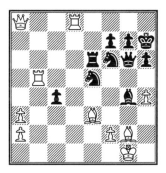

So – Carlsen
Internet 2020
Black to move

Black passed up the safe 30...♕f5 for **30...♘e8**. Why did he do this and how should White reply?

72.

Tartakower – Fine
Kemeri 1937
White to move

Black wants to play ...♗f5, but 19 ♘g3 allows 19...♘xd4!. What is best?

73.

Van der Wiel – Sax
Plovdiv 1983
Black to move

Black chose **16...b5**. What is the best reply?

74.

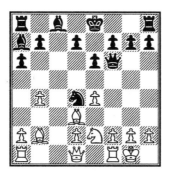

Baklan – Cherniaev
Istanbul 2003
White to move

Black got into a diagonal pin with his last move, 12…♕f6. How do you exploit this?

75.

Navara – Howell
Internet 2020
White to move

What should White do?

76.

Makogonov – Geller
Tbilisi 1951
White to move

White can stop a good Black idea and threaten his own tactic. How?

77.

Williams – Ratnesan
Hastings 2019-20
White to move

White has two ways of winning. Find both.

78.

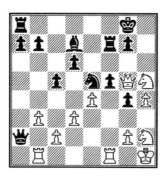

Muzychuk – Dzagnidze
Women's Grand Prix 2020
White to move

How should White proceed?

79.

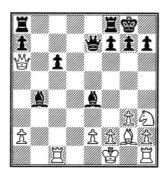

Svidler – Giri
Internet 2020
Black to move

Keep White from untangling his pieces.

Chapter Seven:
How Can I Improve My Pieces?

It is no secret that you will be able to play better if you can calculate better. But you will make greater progress by learning to visualize.

Visualizing is short-cut calculating. It leaves the opponent's moves out of the evaluation.

Calculating is "What happens if I go there and he goes here and then I go there…?"

Visualizing is "What if my pieces are there and there?"

Bobby Fischer was great at calculating – and superb at visualizing.

Fischer – Barcza
Stockholm 1962
White to move

Among the spectators who watched this game was Russian grandmaster Alexander Kotov. In his influential book *Think Like a Grandmaster*, Kotov advocated a rigorous system of analysis. A player must carefully calculate all of the candidate moves in a "tree of variations," he declared. He conceded this can require quite a lot of time.

Kotov was stunned when Fischer took only a few seconds to play his next four moves. The position wasn't tactical enough for Fischer to be worried about Black's moves.

For example, 27 ♖d1 is common-sense chess. Black's only active idea is 27…♘a4. After 28 ♖d2 protects the b2-pawn, Black would have to retreat 28…♘c5 or 28…♖b8 to defend his own b7-pawn.

For example, 28…♖b8 29 ♗d1 ♘c5 30 ♔f1 and ♖d6. This is the extent of the tactics in the position.

Fischer was freed to think in general terms: Where would my rook be placed best? Probably on b4, where it would threaten the b6-pawn. Therefore, **27 ♖d1 ♔f8 28 ♖d4!**.

Black countered **28... ♖c7** so he could meet ♖b4 with ...♞d7.

White to move

Fischer might have tried to exploit Black's last move with 29 ♖d8+ and 29...♔e7 30 ♖b8. But he would have to calculate 30... ♞a4, for example.

Fischer's pragmatism took over. Why calculate an unclear future when he was certain of good winning chances once his rook landed on b4? He continued **29 h3 f5 30 ♖b4! ♞d7**.

Again he could have turned on his remarkable powers of calculation and tried to force matters with 31 ♗d1. The idea is 32 ♗a4 followed by ♗xd7 and ♖xb6.

But Fischer could visualize instead: What about my king? It's doing nothing on g1.Where would it work best? Most likely in the center, perhaps on d4, where it cannot be checked.

Since Black's knight and rook are tied to the defense of pawns, he could play his next moves with hardly any calculation, **31 ♔f1 ♔e7 32 ♔e2 ♔d8 33 ♖b5 g6 34 ♔e3 ♔c8 35 ♔d4 ♔b8**.

White to move

Two of Fischer's three pieces are much better placed than they were eight moves ago. This is an obvious sign of progress.

It is also a hint about the third piece, his bishop. Using it takes some calculating because, for example, 36 ♗d5 would get complicated after 36...f6 37 ♗g8 ♖c8! and 38 ♗xh7 ♘e5.

Instead, he temporized, **36 ♔d5 ♖c6 37 ♔d4 ♖e6**, and then tried to expose the b7-pawn to a double attack, **38 a4 ♔c7 39 a5** (39...bxa5 40 ♖xb7+).

The win did not become evident until after **39...♖d6+ 40 ♗d5 ♔c8 41 axb6 f6 42 ♔e3 ♘xb6 43 ♗g8! ♔c7 44 ♖c5+ ♔b8 45 ♗xh7**.

Flowing Moves

Fischer made chess look easy. In many of his games the moves seem to flow as if in a continuous stream that grows in size until the enemy defenses are overwhelmed.

There is no single secret to doing this. But there is basic advice: Try to put your pieces on better squares, one piece at a time.

If this sounds too simple, it is. Well-placed pieces don't always produce a winning plan or even threats. But this advice works much more often than it fails.

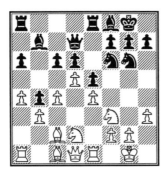

Hübner – Portisch
Brussels 1986
White to move

White can ask himself sophisticated questions about pawns, such as, "Should I play dxc6?" and "Is now the right time for that?"

Or he can ask, "Should I play a4-a5 now or later?"

The answers don't come easily, even to masters. But White can be more certain about his pieces.

A better question is, "What should I do with my knights?" It is easier to find better squares for them right now than for the c1-bishop and a1-rook.

One idea is to post the d2-knight on g3 or e3 after 17 ♘f1.

White preferred to improve his other knight first, **17 ♘h2 ♛c7 18 ♘g4!**.

Black to move

His idea was to prompt 18...♘xg4 so that 19 hxg4! would reinforce the f5-square. Then it would be a more secure future home for the other knight (♘f1-g3-f5).

Black can interrupt this plan with 19...cxd5 20 cxd5 ♖ac8, by threatening ...♛xc2.

But then 21 ♘c4! followed by ♗e3 and ♖c1 would allow White to coordinate his pieces.

Instead, Black should try to make better use of his own minor pieces. One plan is 18...♘d7 followed by ...♘c5.Then ...♗c8-d7 would get more use out of the bishop.

Instead, he tried **18...♗e7**. This bishop can seek play on g5 after ...♘xg4. Or it could try to seize the other good dark-square diagonal later with ...♗d8-b6.

The middlegame unfolded with **19 ♘f1! cxd5 20 cxd5 ♘xg4 21 hxg4.**

167

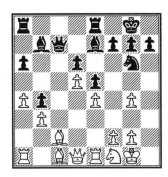

Black to move

Black's pieces would get into a traffic jam after 21...♖ac8 22 ♗d3 ♗d8 23 a5!.

He can avert this with 22...a5. But it allows White to improve his light-squared bishop with 23 ♗b5!.

After 23...♖f8 24 ♘e3 ♗d8 25 ♘c4 Black's bishop can't reach b6.

Instead, Black improved both of his bishops with **21...♗c8 22 ♘e3 ♗g5** and traded one of them off, **23 ♘f5 ♗xc1 24 ♖xc1**.

His last chance to improve a piece significantly was ...♘f8-d7-c5!.

This would plug up the c-file, which has gone from being a Black strength to a White strength.

But it was too late. After 24...♘f8 25 ♗d3 ♕b8, White can reply 26 ♖c6 with a dominating position.

Black found nothing better than **24...♕d8** and **25 ♗d3 ♘e7**.

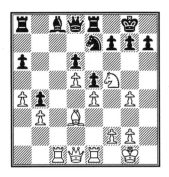

White to move

It was time for White to make his heavy pieces matter via **26 ♕d2 ♖b8 27 ♖c2!** and ♖ec1.

168

If Black defends his a6-pawn with …a5, he allows another White piece to improve, ♗b5!.

So far, White could have played his moves with very little calculation. At no point did he have to consider a Black reply that would trigger a dangerous three-move – or even two-move – sequence.

This changed after **27…♘xf5 28 gxf5 f6 29 ♖ec1 ♖e7** when he chose **30 ♖c6!.**

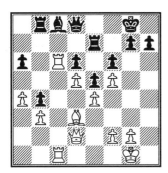

Black to move

He could play this move with confidence because he saw 30…♗b7 can be met by 31 ♗xa6! ♗xc6 32 dxc6. He would win after ♗b7 or ♗b5, followed by ♕xb4 and the advance of his three passed queenside pawns.

The rest was interesting chiefly by the way White improved his final piece, the king:

30…♖a7 31 ♕e2 a5 32 ♗b5 ♗b7 33 ♖c7 ♖c8 34 ♕c4 ♖aa8 35 f3 ♔f8 36 ♔f2 ♖ab8 37 ♔e3! g6 38 ♗d7 ♖xc7 39 ♕xc7 ♕xc7 40 ♖xc7 ♗a6 41 ♗e6 ♖b7 42 ♖c6 ♗f1 43 ♖xd6 ♗c4 44 ♖d8+ resigns.

There are Black moves you can criticize after Move 17. But the basic reason for his loss is, from then on, White kept finding ways to improve his pieces and Black did not.

Optimum

Improving a piece can be a two-step process, as it was in the Fischer game. First, you figure out which piece should be moved next. Second, you find the optimum square for it.

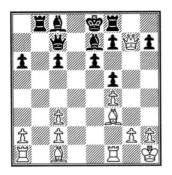

Velimirović –Damjanović
Sombor 1972
White to move

The first step is the easier one here. General principles indicate White's c1-bishop should move next, if only to connect his rooks. White would have the upper hand after 18 ♗e3 and then 18...c5 19 ♖ab1, for instance.

But is 18 ♗e3 the best move? You can get the right answer after a lot of calculating. But much simpler is asking which is the optimum square for the bishop.

If you free your imagination from "If I go there, and he goes there...", you may see e5 is by far the best.

Once you realize this, you can look for a route for the bishop to get there. The fastest is **18 c4!** and ♗b2-e5.

Black can stop ♗b2 with 18...♛b6. But you don't have to look far to see that 19 ♗d2 and ♗c3-e5! would get the bishop where it belongs.

Play went **18...c5 19 ♗b2**.

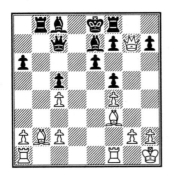

Black to move

White's advantage would be close to decisive after 20 ♖ad1. Then 21 ♗e5 is threatened.

Black would be paralyzed after 20...♗d6 21 ♗e5 ♗xe5 22 fxe5, followed by doubling rooks on the d-file, for example.

He tried **19...♗b7 20 ♗e5 ♗d6**. This puts up a defense in case of 21 ♖ad1 ♗xe5 22 fxe5 ♗xf3 and ...♖d8!.

But he was lost after **21 ♗xd6 ♕xd6 22 ♖ad1**.

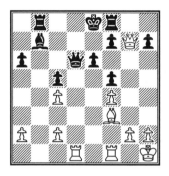

Black to move

The dark-squared bishops are gone but Black's heavy pieces are outgunned.

For example, 22...♕b6 23 ♖b1 ♕c7 24 ♕b2! wins.

The game went **22...♕c7 23 ♖fe1!**, and Black did not have a good answer to the threat of 24 ♖xe6+! (24...fxe6 25 ♕xc7).

He tried **23...♗c8**. White won after **24 ♕f6**, although 24 ♖e3! and 25 ♖ed3 would have saved time.

Second Moves

The benefits of asking "How can I improve my pieces" become evident early in a game, when it is time to move a knight or bishop for the second time.

The first move of a minor piece is usually predetermined by the opening you chose. When the middlegame begins, you have to start thinking about their optimum squares.

171

Unzicker – Taimanov
Stockholm 1952
Black to move

Black's queen exerts latent pressure on the e4-pawn. He will maximize the power of his rooks after ...♖fc8.

What about his minor pieces? His c6-knight blocks the long diagonal. This inspired **16...♘d8!** and ...♘e6.

If this knight gets to c5, White will be hard pressed to defend his e- and c-pawns.

White saw this coming. He safeguarded his pawns with **17 ♗d3 ♘e6 18 ♖c1**.

After **18...♖fc8 19 ♘h2** he might continue ♘f1-g3 with a secure position.

Black to move

In the next chapter we will consider the checklist question "Will my position get better?" That is, get better with routine, quiet moves. This is important to ask because the best policy may be to take an irrevocable step instead.

Here Black considered the irrevocable step of 19...d5. After 20 exd5 ♗xd5 his bishop would take aim at g2.

This would favor him after, for example, 21 ♗f1! ♘e4! 22 ♘xe4 ♗xe4 and 23 c4 ♗g5!.

Many masters prefer to keep a pawn structure unchanged until they have gotten the most out of it with routine moves that improve pieces.

One way is 19...♘f4.

Black chose to get more out of his other knight, **19...♘d7** and ...♘dc5!,

The game continued **20 ♘hf1 ♘dc5! 21 ♘g3 g6.**

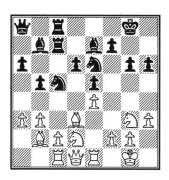

White to move

Now the e7-bishop is poised to make its second move of the game, and it has a good choice. It may go to g5 or to h4 (with ...♗xg3 and ...♕a7 in mind).

White anticipated ...♗xg3 as well as ...♘f4 with **22 ♘e2.**

But Black still had ways to improve pieces and did so with **22...♗g5! 23 ♘c3 ♘d4.**

Note that he has not made a forcing move since the first diagram. The only calculation that seems necessary was evaluating 19...d5.

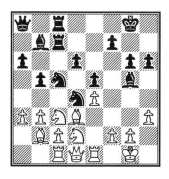

White to move

But with his pieces at maximum utility, he was primed to force matters, such as with 24...♘xd3 25 cxd3 a5 and ...b4.

White hoped to trade one of the most obnoxious Black pieces with **24 ♘cb1** and ♗xd4.

When Black asks "What is wrong with his move?" he sees it made **24...d5** stronger.

He won after **25 exd5?** (better is 25 ♘c3) **♘xd3 26 cxd3 ♖xc1 27 ♗xc1 ♗xd5 28 f3 ♖c2 29 a4 b4 30 ♔h1 ♕c6**. White resigned because of ...♘f5/...♗f4/...♘g3+, for example.

Black overlooked another drawback of 24 ♘cb1. It allowed 24...♘xd3 25 cxd3 ♖xc1 26 ♗xc1 ♖c2!, with the idea of ...♕c8/...♖xc1! or ...d5.

Outdated

As the opening blends into the middlegame, the knights, rooks and bishops typically improve in different ways:

Knights try to advance to outpost squares. This usually means squares on the fourth to sixth ranks on the c- to f-files.

Rooks often improve laterally, by sliding along the first rank to open files.

But finding the optimum squares for bishops tends to be harder. They are routinely developed according to a book opening. In the middlegame they may find themselves on outdated diagonals.

Razuvaev – Levitt
Reykjavik 1990
Black to move

White's bishop seems well placed at a3, where it stops ...0-0.

When Black played **14...0-0-0**, White could appreciate his reasoning. In addition to connecting his rooks, Black can seek counterplay from ...e5 or ...♘e5.

But when White looked for other significant changes made by 14...0-0-0, he realized his bishop might be misplaced on a3.

It still enjoyed control of a nice diagonal leading to f8. But there were no targets there.

This prompted **15 ♗e7! ♖de8 16 ♗h4.**

Black to move

White had canceled the ...♘e5 trick and made ...e5 more problematic in view of the reply ♗g3. But his maneuver was more than prophylactic.

When Black asks, "What does he want?" – he would see 17 ♗g3. But he might also appreciate 17 a5!.

Then his queen cannot go to a5 after 18 ♗g3. White could follow with ♕f4 and begin to threaten his king.

This would tell Black what White had realized two moves earlier: The g3-b8 diagonal has become much more important than the a3-f8 diagonal.

Black could anticipate danger with 16...♕a5 17 ♗g3 e5!, but he chose **16...f6**.

He ran into trouble on that diagonal after **17 a5! ♖hf8 18 ♗g3**, and eventually lost after **18...e5 19 f4** (or 19 a6 b5 20 ♗e2 and later ♗g4).

Structural Change

When you weigh changes in a middlegame pawn structure, the most significant criteria is how it affects your pieces.

You already know this when you open a file so your rooks can perform better. Evaluating the future of minor pieces is more of a challenge.

Trifunović – Stoltz
Prague 1946
Black to move

White stands well, partly because his knight is better placed than Black's.

Black could change this by preparing ...♗xd5. But then cxd5! would allow White's bishop to dominate the light squares on the queenside with ♗b5 or ♗a6.

A better change in the pawn structure is 18...e6. This would drive White's knight back at the cost of weakening Black's d6-pawn. Black would then be passive but solid, after ...♖d7 and ...♖fd8.

But the best structural change was **18...e5!**.

White to move

Black's knight will be at least as good as White's after …♘d4. The d6-pawn may look just as weak as it would after 18…e6. But it isn't vulnerable because White rooks can't threaten it.

The rook that may benefit the most from 18…e5 is the one at f8. It can support an …f5! break.

White tried to exploit …♘d4 with **19 ♖c3 ♘d4! 20 ♖a3**. Once Black moved his knight from c6, the a7-pawn cannot be easily defended by other pieces (20…♖a8 21 ♘c7 ♖ac8 22 ♘b5).

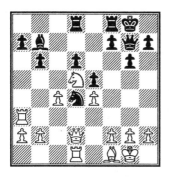

Black to move

But Black happily got rid of his bishop, **20...♗xd5!**. With his pawn on e5, his d4-knight is better than the White bishop, and he would have kingside play after 21 cxd5 f5!.

White played the more optimistic **21 exd5 ♖d7 22 f4**.

Then 22…f5 would give White's rooks something to do. They can pressure the e5-pawn with 23 ♖e1! and ♖ae3.

Black would like to reply …e4. But his knight would be undefended, with nowhere to retreat after ♖d1!.

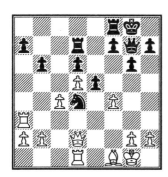

Black to move

However, **22...f6!** reinforced the knight. Then Black had the only major source of play for either side, ...g5!.

His position steadily improved, **23 ♖e3 g5! 24 fxg5 fxg5 25 ♗d3 ♖f4 26 ♖f1 ♖df7**, and he eventually won.

Dead End

An amateur often feels frustrated when he reaches an apparent dead end in the middlegame. He can't explain why.

His pieces are well placed. By all measures, he should have a substantial advantage. But he sees there is no obvious way to make progress. What went wrong?

Nothing is wrong. The problem often lies in the words "well placed."

Ragozin – Geller
Kiev 1950
White to move

All of White's pieces occupy squares that look good. But one is not doing much: the knight at c3.

What is the ideal square for it? If you visualize – don't try to calculate – you can see it would inflict fatal damage on f6.

Yes, this is at least six moves away. But after **22 ♘ce2** and g4-g5 the knight had a clear path, ♘c1-d3-f2-g4-f6.

There is another way to decisively improve the knight after 22 ♘ce2. This is harder to visualize. After ♔h1, White can play ♘g1-f3-g5. Then the threat of ♘xh7 would prompt ...h6. White could then win with ♘gf3 and f4-f5.

Slow maneuvering wouldn't work if Black had serious counterplay. But 22...b4, for instance, can be met by 23 b3!.

This would cost the b4-pawn or put his queen on a bad square, 23...♕c5 (24 c3! threatens ♘xe6!).

The game went **22...♕c7 23 ♘c1 a5 24 ♘d3 ♗a6 25 g5**.

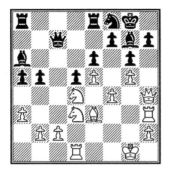

Black to move

Now, for example, 25...♖ab8 26 ♘f2 b4 is lost after 27 ♘g4!, followed by 28 ♘f6+ ♔h8 29 ♕xh7+! or 28...♗xf6 29 gxf6 and ♕h6-g7 mate.

Black resorted to **25...♗h8 26 ♘f2 h5 27 gxh6 ♘h7**, but it was as bad as it looked. He resigned after **28 ♖g3 b4 29 axb4 axb4 30 ♕g4 ♘f8 31 h4 ♖eb8 32 h5! ♗c8 33 ♘h3 ♖a6 34 ♘g5! gxh5 35 h7+**.

His Worst Piece

As we've seen, it often pays to reverse a checklist question, such as asking yourself, "What is *my* weakest point?" In the next diagram, White should ask "How can he improve *his* pieces?"

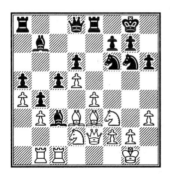

Karjakin – Caruana
Sao Paulo 2012
White to move

After White chose **23 ♕d1** Black can ask two checklist questions. First: What does he want?

Perhaps he sought to smooth out his piece placement by means of ♕c2 and ♘f1-g3, and then offer a bishop trade with ♗d2.

The second question is: What could be wrong with a move as quiet 23 ♕d1? The answer is it makes **23...♗a6!** possible.

This significantly improves the bishop. In addition, 24 ♗xa6 ♖xa6 would make the e4-pawn the weakest point on the board. It would be doomed after another Black piece improvement, ...♖a7! and ...♖ae7.

Therefore White chose **24 ♗c2.**

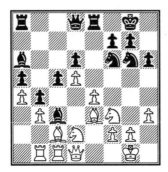

Black to move

But **24...♖a7!** and ...♖ae7 was still a strong idea.

There was no way for White to safely add protection to his e4-pawn. If he moves his f3-knight, so he can prepare f2-f3, Black immediately wins the pawn with 25...♗xd2 and 26...♘xe4.

He was grasping at straws with **25 ♔h2 ♖ae7 26 g4.** Black had a choice of ways to win. He opted for **26...♘xe4! 27 ♘xe4 ♖xe4 28 ♗xe4 ♖xe4** because he had 29...♕f6 followed by ...♘f4.

The game ended with **29 ♕c2 ♕e7 30 ♖g1? ♖xe3! 31 fxe3 ♕xe3 32 ♖bf1 ♗e2 33 ♕f5 ♗d3 34 ♕d7 ♗e5+ 35 ♔h1 ♗e4! 36 ♕e8+ ♘f8 White resigns**.

What To Remember

Forming a middlegame or endgame plan may seem like a daunting task. But planning is little more than visualizing what your current position would look like if you improve specific pieces.

Visualizing can begin as soon as you run out of the opening moves you know. Be particularly careful when weighing the second move of a minor piece. A knight or bishop may have appeared well-placed but this impression is often out of date when the middlegame intensifies.

Quiz

80.

Caruana – Shankland
US Championship 2016
White to move

Black's last move, 24...b3, handed White a powerful plan. Which?

81.

Adams – Bacrot
Leon 2001
White to move

Which piece is best at targeting the weakest Black point?

82.

Xie Jun – Larsen
Monaco 1994
White to move

How should White continue?

83.

Dzindzichashvili – Furman
Baku 1972
Black to move

How can Black seek an advantage?

84.

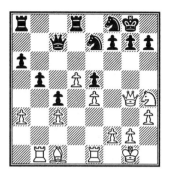

Geller – Padevsky
Dresden 1959
White to move

Neither ♖e3-g3 nor ♗h6 would promise White much after ...♘eg6. What should he do?

85.

Topalov – Ivanchuk
Sofia 2008
Black to move

Find the best of Black's promising options.

86.

Galliamova – Prokopchuk
Novgorod 1999
White to move

White would have little to show after 32 ♕h7+ ♔f8. What is best?

87.

Nepomniachtchi – Artemiev
Internet 2020
White to move

To finish off, does White need one more attacking piece, such as 41 ♖d3 and ♖f3?

88.

Zsu. Polgar – Lau
Polanica Zdroj 1991
White to move

How should White continue?

89.

Leko – Giri
Internet 2020
White to move

What is the follow up to **43 ♗f1** ?

90.

Ciocâltea – Gligorić
Moscow 1956
Black to move

Is there a good alternative to 20...♗d7 and ...♖b8/...b5 ?

Chapter Eight:
Will My Position Get Better?

This is one of the most difficult checklist questions because it requires you to predict the future. To be exact, two futures.

One future is what happens if you play relatively quiet moves. The other is what happens if you take an irrevocable step.

This could mean anything from sacrificing a rook to exchanging your best piece or advancing a key pawn.

Taimanov – Karpov
Moscow 1973
Black to move

Will Black's position get better with routine moves?

Anatoly Karpov quickly realized it would not: It would get worse if he allowed 18 c4! followed by 19 ♗f4!.

This told him his next move was especially important. It was likely to be one of the three or four points in a game when finding the best move makes a huge difference.

Karpov had a choice. He could take the sting out of c3-c4 with 17...♘e4.

The winning chances would be roughly balanced after 18 c4 ♘xd2 and, for example, 19...♕b7 and ...♖fc8.

But there was a more consequential option – the equivalent of burning a bridge.

He stopped c3-c4 by offering a pawn sacrifice, **17...♖c4!**.

White to move

Should White accept the pawn?

He can find an answer by deeply calculating 18 ♕xa7 ♕c6 and Black's threat to trap the queen with 19...♖a8.

The queen would escape with 20 ♕a3. There would be lots of follow-up moves, for both sides, to analyze.

But more practical is asking the same checklist question Black asked: Will my position get better with routine moves? That is, by declining the pawn.

Mark Taimanov came to the same answer as Karpov: No.

After 18 ♕b3? ♕c6, Taimanov could foresee – by visualizing, not calculating – how he would be under strong queenside pressure. Karpov could improve his chances with moves such as ...♖fc8, ...b5 and...a6.

Taimanov could not be certain, but it seemed likely that eventually Black would win the c3- or a2-pawn.

Therefore, he chose **18 ♕xa7! ♕c6 19 ♕a3**.

There were no good forcing moves to consider, so a lot of maneuvering followed: **19...♖c8 20 h3 h6 21 ♖b1 ♖a4 22 ♕b3 ♘d5 23 ♖dc1 ♖c4 24 ♖b2**.

Black to move

188

By now it was clear that 17...♖c4! was a good decision. Black can regain his pawn just about any time he wants, with ...♘xc3.

A capture is another kind of irrevocable step. It burns bridges. Is now the right time?

Getting the right answer requires a lot more calculation than 17...♖c4 did. It starts with 24...♘xc3 and then 25 ♗xc3 ♖xc3 26 ♖xc3 ♕xc3 27 ♕xc3 ♖xc3.

It was difficult to see that far ahead and believe Black would have a significant advantage. In fact, analysis later showed how 28 ♘e5! ♘xe5 29 dxe5 would leave a drawish rook endgame (29...♖a3 30 ♖xb6 ♖xa2).

Karpov thought his position would get better with quiet moves. He started with **24...f6**, to rule out ♘e5.

Then came **25 ♖e1 ♔f7 26 ♕d1 ♘f8 27 ♖b3 ♘g6 28 ♕b1 ♖a8 29 ♖e4 ♖ca4 30 ♖b2 ♘f8 31 ♕d3 ♖c4 32 ♖e1 ♖a3 33 ♕b1 ♘g6 34 ♖c1**.

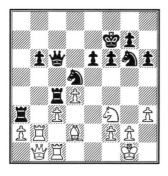

Black to move

Can Black put his pieces on better squares? Probably not.

If he piles up on the a-file (...♕a8/...♖ca4) he allows c3-c4!. And 34...♘gf4 backfires after 35 ♗xf4 ♘xf4 36 ♖xb6.

It was time for another bridge-burning decision. He could have cashed in on his pressure with **34...♖axc3!**. Then 35 ♗xc3 ♘xc3 would threaten ...♘xb1 as well as ...♘e2+.

However, the game became sloppy with **34...♘xc3? 35 ♕d3?** (35 ♖xb6!) **♘e2+ 36 ♕xe2 ♖xc1+ 37 ♗xc1 ♕xc1+ 38 ♔h2 ♖xf3?! 39 gxf3 ♘h4**.

White resigned. This was the worst move of the game because 40 d5! might have drawn after 40 ...exd5 41 ♖b4.

But this should not detract from what the game teaches about urgency.

Both players recognized when to burn bridges (17...♖c4! and 18 ♕xa7!) and when not to (24...f6).

When You Can Wait

Karpov could afford to wait nearly 20 moves between taking irrevocable steps because he had what is often called a "bind." This is when you have severely limited your opponent's options. He has little or no counterplay.

How long you *can* wait will be determined by how long you can maintain the bind. How long you *should* wait will be determined by how much you can improve your chances before delivering a decisive blow.

Alatortsev – Lyublinsky
Moscow 1950
White to move

White's position looks so good, he can begin his search for that blow. The tactical idea that stands out is ♗xf6 followed by ♘d5.

At first, this looks like the right time: 25 ♗xf6 ♕xf6 26 ♘d5 sets up a paralyzing pin after 26...♗xd5 27 ♗xd5+ ♘e6.

Black cannot survive 28 ♕c4 followed by 29 ♖a2 and 30 ♖ae2.

But he can evade the pin, with 27...♔h8! (instead of 27....♘e6??). Then the tactical trail runs dry, e.g. 28 ♔g2 g6 29 ♖h1+ ♔g7.

However, the ♗xf6 option is not going away. White can store it in his memory while he relies on principled moves.

He can wait, with **25 ♖e2!**.

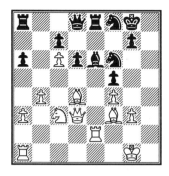

Black to move

What does White want? Of course, it is ♖ae1, with the threat of ♘d5.

Moving the bishop would lose the f5-pawn or allow 25...♗c8 26 ♗xf6! gxf6 27 ♘d5, for example.

Black's best chance was **25...♕e7!** and ...♕f7.

White might be lured into 26 ♘d5 ♘xd5 27 ♗xd5. Then 27...♕f7 would give Black reason to hope.

But there was no reason for White to use the ♘d5 idea until he saw it was decisive. He chose **26 ♖ae1!**.

Black got out of the e-file pin with **26...♕f7** and threatened 27...♗c4.

White to move

White can continue to look for quiet, solid moves, such as 27 ♖e3 and 28 ♕e2.

This requires a surprising amount of calculation, for example, of 27...♗c4 28 ♕xf5 ♖xe3 29 ♖xe3 ♘e6 (30 ♗xf6 ♘d4!).

191

But once he played 26 ♖ae1, White knew his pieces were approaching their maximum utility. It made sense to investigate the forcing idea he had mentally stored, **27 ♗xf6! ♕xf6 28 ♘d5.**

He saw 28...♗xd5?? now loses to 29 ♗xd5+! and ♖xe8.

Black had to play **28...♕f7.**

White to move

Black would lose at least a pawn if he moves his queen, bishop or knight (29...♘g6 30 ♘xc7!).

But White has no forcing moves that improve his chances. Black is so lacking in counterplay, White can visualize – not calculate – the quiet moves that might win:

He can visualize a kingside plan of invading the h-file, with ♖h2, ♔f2 and ♖eh1.

He can also visualize a slower queenside plan of a3-a4, b4-b5 and b5-b6, to create a winning passed c-pawn.

He decided on another plan, based on ♕d4, ♖h1 and ♗h5. It began with **29 ♔f2 ♔h8 30 ♕d4 ♔g8 31 ♖e3 ♖eb8 32 ♖h1.**

Black to move

There was no good answer to 33 ♗h5 (33...g6 34 ♘f6+). Black played **32...a5 33 ♗h5 ♗xd5 34 ♗xf7+ ♔xf7** before resigning.

When You Can't Wait

Black was doomed in that game by his passive pieces. He could see a worsening future after 25 ♖e2 but could not stop it.

When a defender's pieces are not passive, he has more options, including burning bridges.

Petrosian – Borisenko, Moscow 1950

1 d4 ♘f6 2 c4 g6 3 ♘c3 ♗g7 4 e4 d6 5 f3 0-0 6 ♗g5 c5 7 d5 h6 8 ♗e3 e6 9 dxe6 ♗xe6 10 ♗d3 ♘c6 11 ♘ge2 ♘e5 12 b3

Black to move

Given time – that is, if Black plays quiet moves – White can continue with 0-0, ♕d2 and ♖ad1. His superior pawn structure will harden into a permanent positional plus.

Black realized three things: (1) He should avert this future, (2) He needs tactics to do it and (3) The best tactical source is a sacrifice, ...b5.

A little calculation told him that preparing ...b5 with 12...a6 would be too slow.

He would not have enough compensation after 13 0-0 b5 14 cxb5 ♘xd3 15 ♕xd3 axb5 16 ♕xb5, for instance.

This told him, "Now or never." He played **12...b5!** and threatened to win the c4-pawn.

193

White to move

His main tactical idea is subtle – the a1-rook will be hanging in key variations.

For example, 13 ♘d5? allows 13...♗xd5 14 exd5 ♘xd5!.

Then 15 cxd5 ♘xd3+ 16 ♕xd3 ♗xa1 wins for Black.

Little better for White is 13 cxb5? d5!. Then 14 ♗xc5? dxe4! powerfully threatens ...♘xd3+.

Also bad is 14 exd5 ♘xd5 15 ♘xd5 and then 15...♘xd3+ 16 ♕xd3 ♗xa1 or just 15...♗xd5.

This left Tigran Petrosian with **13 ♘xb5**.

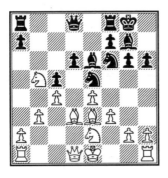

Black to move

The situation remains urgent for Black. He cannot wait to play his next forcing move.

One idea is 13...♘fg4!, to attack the e3-bishop and open more of the g7-a1 diagonal.

194

White would have nothing better than 14 fxg4. Chances would be roughly equal after Black grabs the Exchange, 14...♘xd3+ 15 ♕xd3 ♗xa1.

He preferred **13...♘xd3+ 14 ♕xd3 ♘xe4!**, again based on his main tactical idea (...♗xa1).

Another balanced middlegame would be ahead after 15 0-0 ♗xa1 16 ♖xa1 a6!.

Petrosian defended with the most principled – and practical – move, **15 ♖d1!.**

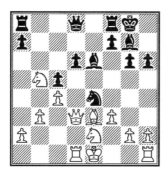

Black to move

It was practical because, by keeping his extra Exchange, he put the onus on Black. Black failed the test with **15...♕a5+?** and **16 ♗d2 ♘xd2 17 ♕xd2**.

He lost the endgame that followed **17...♕b6 18 ♕xd6 ♖fd8 19 ♕xb6**.

After the game, it was found that 15...a6! would have offered Black equal chances.

For example, 16 ♘xd6 ♕a5+ 17 ♗d2 ♘xd2 18 ♕xd2 ♕b6! and ...♖ad8. Better is 16 ♘c7! ♕xc7 17 fxe4 and 17...♖ae8 or 17...♕e7 and ...♗g4.

The bottom line: Black correctly saw a bad trend at move 12 and correctly saw a window of opportunity based on ...b5!. He changed the trend but lost because of a later mistake.

Windows

Black's window was only open briefly after move 12. More often, a window can be kept open by making accurate moves.

Ponomariev – van Wely
World Cup 2005
White to move

What does Black want? Getting his king to safety is priority Number 1.

Nothing harmful will come to White after 15 ♖e1, 15 ♖c1 or 15 ♘e5. But these moves promise no advantage after 15...0-0!.

The only way for White to prove his position is superior is by **15 ♕a4+!**.

This superiority would be visible after 15...♘c6 16 d5! because the Black king is kept in the firing zone. For example, 16...exd5 17 ♖fe1+ ♗e6 18 ♘d4. Or 17 ♕a3 ♗e6 18 ♘b5.

To avoid this, Black chose **15...♗d7**.

White to move

To keep his window wide open, White needs to be careful. After 16 ♕b4?! Black has 16...a5!.

Then 17 ♕xb7 ♗c6 18 ♕-moves ♗xf3 makes White's king the more vulnerable one.

But with the more accurate **16 ♕a3!** he denies Black tactical tricks, while preventing his king from fleeing (16...0-0? 17 ♕xe7).

Black needs an accurate response before 17 ♖fe1 is followed by 18 d5! (18...♘xd5 19 ♖e5).

He anticipated this with **16...♘d5.**

White to move

The window would be closing after 17 ♘xd5 ♕xd5 18 ♖fe1 f6!, for example.

Or after 18 ♖ac1 ♗c6 19 ♖c5 ♕d6 and ...0-0.

White found another forcing idea, **17 ♘e5!**.

He threatened to win with 18 ♘xd5 exd5 19 ♖fe1 ♗e6 20 ♖ac1 and ♖c7.

Black's best try was 17...♗c6. But he played **17...♘xc3? 18 bxc3 ♕g5.**

White to move

One more time: What does Black want? To play 19...♕e7!.

White could keep an advantage with 19 ♘xd7 ♔xd7, provided he continues 20 d5!.

But he did not want to liquidate a major positional asset – the great knight – so quickly.

He found **19 ♖ab1!** and the threat of ♖xb7 wins.

Then 19...b5 makes 20 ♘xd7 ♔xd7 21 d5! stronger (21...exd5 22 ♖xb5; 21...♕xd5 22 ♖fd1).

White won after **19...♗c8 20 ♖fe1 ♕e7 21 ♕a4+ ♔f8 22 d5! h5?** (22...♔g8 23 ♖bd1 and 24 d6) **23 ♖bd1 dxe5 24 ♘g6+** and ♖xe7.

Enduring Windows

If it is unlikely that a window will be shut quickly, you can take your time to use your best tactical or positional idea. It may work on the next move, but it might be just as good a move later.

Konstantinopolsky – Kholmov
Tartu 1950
White to move

Masters will recognize a tactical pattern and a thematic sacrifice, ♘d5.

Here 14 ♘d5! exd5 works in its simplest form. White can get his knight back with 15 ♗xf6 ♗xf6 16 cxd5 and dxc6.

Much better is 15 cxd5! ♘xd5 16 ♘d4 and ♘xc6.

Black can decline the knight offer with 14...♕d8. He would be positionally worse after 15 ♘xe7+ ♕xe7 16 b4, for example.

Yet White played **14 e4.**

Black to move

Did he fail to recognize the pattern? Not necessarily.

The sacrifice is strengthened by 14 e4 because White will have the option of recapturing exd5 after 15 ♘d5 exd5. Then he would threaten ♖xe7.

For example, 14...♕b7 15 ♘d5! exd5 16 exd5 ♗e8 17 b4.

Or even 17 ♘d4 ♕d7 18 ♖xe7! ♕xe7 19 ♘f5 ♕d8 20 ♕g5.

Play went **14...♖d8 15 ♘d5!**.

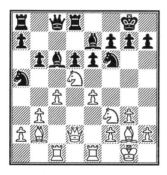

Black to move

Now 15...♕d7 would lose a piece, 16 ♘xf6+ ♗xf6 17 ♗xf6 gxf6 18 b4 ♘b7 19 b5.

Black fell back on **15...♗xd5 16 cxd5**.

But then he saw how dreadful 16...♕b8 17 dxe6 fxe6 17 b4 ♘b7 18 ♘d4 is.

He was lost after **16...♕d7 17 ♗h3!** and resigned after **17...h5 18 dxe6 fxe6 19 ♕g5 ♘c6 20 ♕g6 ♖dc8 21 ♖xc6 ♖xc6 22 ♘g5 d5 23 ♕f7+ ♔h8 24 ♗xf6**.

Let's go back to the previous diagram. Was there a way for Black to discourage 15 ♘d5 ?

Yes, with 14...♕d7. But after 15 ♕e2 (threatening 16 b4 ♘b7 17 b5) ♗b7 16 ♖cd1 (threatening 17 e5) Black would be in bad shape.

For instance, 16...♕c8 17 ♗a3 or 16...♘e8 17 e5.

Therefore, 14 ♘d5! was good. But so was 14 e4!.

Two-Way Windows

When you open a window in your house, it benefits the person who opened it. You get the fresh air you wanted.

When a window of opportunity is opened it may benefit both players.

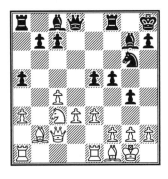

Ribli – Lobron
Bundesliga 1992
Black to move

Will Black's position get better with quiet moves? Perhaps a little, after 19...♗e6 and 19...b6.

But he would remain slightly worse if White sees how 20 ♖ad1 and d3-d4! would favor him.

Even after 19...b6 20 ♖ad1 c5 White can play 21 d4!. For instance, 21...exd4 22 exd4 cxd4 23 ♘b5 and ♘xd4, with advantage.

These scenarios are not exhaustive. But they signaled a bad trend for Black. He got the message and tried to break the trend with **19...♘h4!**.

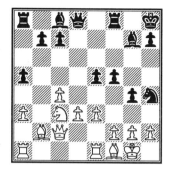

White to move

This should have been a wake-up call to White. What does Black want?

The answer is not obvious. Some computers initially find a big White edge after 20 ♖ad1.

But Black's hidden idea is ...♖a6-h6!. He had seen that White's weakest points are g2 and h2, and they can both be exploited by a knight sacrifice on f3.

This became clearer after **20 ♖ad1?** was met by **20...♖a6!**.

White to move

Panic time. Belatedly White saw the threat of 21...♘f3+! 22 gxf3 gxf3 and the fatal follow-up of ...♖g6+ and ...♕h4.

He tried **21 d4** but was lost after **21...♘f3+! 22 gxf3 gxf3**.

His pieces could not defend the kingside (23 ♘e2 ♕h4! 24 ♘g3 ♖h6 25 h3 f4! and ...♗xh3).

The last moves were **23 dxe5 ♕h4 24 ♘e2 ♖h6 25 h3 fxe2 26 ♕xe2 f4 27 e6 ♖g6+ 28 ♔h2 f3 29 ♕c2 ♕g5 White resigns**.

Let's scroll back to the game's pivotal moment, after 19...♘h4!. White needed to burn his own bridges with 20 d4!.

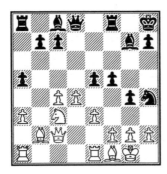

Black to move

With the knight still on g6, Black would have a fine game after 20...f4!.

But on h4, it allowed White to answer 20...f4? with 21 dxe5!. This would favor him after 21...♗xe5 22 ♖ad1 followed by exf4.

Better is 20...exd4. White would win after 21 exd4 ♗xd4? 22 ♘d5! or 21...♕xd4? 22 ♖e7! (and 23 ♖xg7!).

Instead, 21...♖a6 leads to double-edged play after 22 ♘d5.

In other words, Black opened a window of opportunity with 19...♘h4. But White could have exploited the window with 20 d4.

Potential Energy

"Will my position get better?" is often the decisive factor when a player decides to make a sacrifice. The other major kind of bridge-burning step is the liquidation of a positional advantage.

A positional advantage is like potential energy in physics. A player tries to amass potential energy in the form of non-material assets, such as pressure against a target. He may have opportunities to convert them into material, such as an extra pawn.

Knowing when to do this is one of the greatest of chess skills. A master does not liquidate pressure until he thinks he won't get more in return.

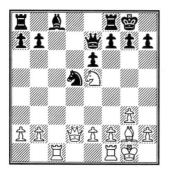

Kasparov – Petrosian
Bugojno 1982
White to move

Garry Kasparov was stockpiling positional assets. He has a rook on an open file and a bishop on the diagonal that matters most.

He can try to cash some assets with 15 ♗xd5. Then 15...exd5 16 ♕xd5 ♗h3 17 ♖fd1 wins a pawn.

But Black has a simple defense, 15...♖d8!.

There is another forcing move, 15 e4. This gives up on ♗xd5 but shows promise after 15...♘b6 16 ♖fd1.

However, White can also see how his chances would be enhanced by quiet, principled moves. The forcing ♗xd5 and e2-e4 ideas were not going away.

He chose **15 ♖fd1!**.

Black to move

His move was also prophylactic. Black could not play his own principled moves because, for example, 15...♖d8 ? 16 e4 and 15...♗d7? 16 ♘xd7 ♕xd7 17 e4 cost a piece.

Petrosian played his own prophylactic move, **15...♞b6**. He had 16...f6 and ...e5 in mind, so he could develop his bishop.

Is there a drawback to 15...♞b6 ? One that comes to mind is White can force a favorable endgame with 16 ♛d6.

But having the more active queen is one of his positional assets. It should not be traded unless there is no good alternative.

Kasparov chose **16 ♛a5!** so that 16...f6 16 ♞c4 ♞xc4 17 ♜xc4 sets up 18 ♜c7!.

Play went **16...g6 17 ♜d3**.

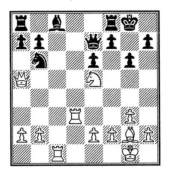

Black to move

You can tell how badly off Black is by finding the tactical flaw in every move that appears constructive.

The obvious ones are 17...♝d7 18 ♝xb7 and 17...♜b8 18 ♛xa7.

But there is also 17...♜d8 18 ♛c5! (18...♛xc5? 19 ♜xd8+).

Petrosian offered a pawn, **17...♞d5**. He would get considerable relief after 18 ♝xd5 exd5 19 ♛xd5 ♝e6 or 19 ♜xd5 ♝e6.

But White's assets – his potential energy – are worth much more than a pawn.

There were no obvious ways to improve his position quietly, so he used his other forcing idea, **18 e4!**.

Clearly 18...♞f6 19 ♜c7 and 18...♛b4 19 ♜xd5! fail.

Play went **18...♞b6 19 ♝f1**.

Black to move

White can see two strong plans:

One is to plant his queen on c5. After a trade of queens, his rook will paralyze Black with ♖c7.

A simpler alternative is based on visualization: Put the queen on b5 and push the a-pawn as far as it will go. Black has no counterplay, so this does not require calculation.

Kasparov took his time, **19...♖e8 20 ♖dd1 ♖f8 21 a3 ♔g7 22 b3 ♔g8 23 a4 ♖d8? 24 ♕c5!**.

Petrosian resigned in view of 24...♕xc5 25 ♖xd8+ ♕f8 26 ♖xf8+ ♔xf8 27 ♖c7.

Buying Out

In sharper positions, a defender may try to buy his way out of pressure by offering more than a pawn. His opponent has to decide whether the price is right, based on the value of his positional assets.

Stohl – Keitlinghaus
Prague 1992
Black to move

205

Black's kingside is badly compromised. Can he survive with routine moves?

Not likely, in view of 20 ♕h5 followed by a sacrifice on h6.

If this doesn't mate by force, White can add a reinforcement, a rook after ♔g2 and ♖h1.

Black tried **19...♘e7!**.

The knight is headed to g8 to defend h6. En route, he is threatening 20...♘xg6.

But there was also a practical point. Black was trying to buy his way out of a likely doomed defense by offering the Exchange.

White to move

White's greatest positional asset is his control of light squares. He would sell it with 20 ♗xa8? ♕xa8.

This severely weakens his attack: 21 ♕g4 or 21 ♕h5 would be double-edged after 21...♖f5! or 21...♗c6!.

But after evaluating this, White should ask, "Will my position improve with routine moves?"

The answer is no. Black threatens his control of light squares with ...♗c6 followed by ...♗xe4.

White can try to preserve his bishop with 20 ♘f4 ♗c6 21 ♗d3.

This looks good. But it is hardly decisive after, say, 21...♗b7 intending 22...♕c6.

White needed to find an alternative with more punch. He chose **20 ♕h5**.

The threat of ♗xh6 forced **20...♘g8**.

White to move

White has another winning plan, g3-g4-g5.

But when he looks at 21 g4?, he sees 21...♗c6!.

Then 22 ♗xc6 ♕xc6 24 g5 ♕f3! turns out poorly.

Analysis of this, and the 21 ♗xa8 buyout, reinforces what White has learned about the position. A successful attack requires light-square control.

He preserved it with **21 ♕h1!**.

Only in retrospect is it obvious. By controlling the h1-a8 diagonal, White wins time for a deadly push of the g-pawn.

Black resigned soon after **21...♖d8 22 g4 ♘a6 23 g5 ♖f5 24 ♗xf5 exf5 25 ♕h5**.

He could have tried to force a bishop trade with 21...♖c8 22 g4! ♘a6 23 g5 ♗c6.

But after 24 gxh6 gxh6 25 ♗xh6 ♗xe4 26 ♗g7+ he is mated.

White needed calculation to make 21 ♕h1 work. But calculation was necessary only after asking the checklist question.

What To Remember

There are pivotal moments in a typical game when it pays to take an irrevocable step. These steps include sacrificing material and accepting sacrifices.

The easiest way to recognizing those moments is to ask yourself whether your chances will improve with routine moves. There are times when you should wait and times when you cannot. A window of opportunity may remain open briefly and it may be exploited by your opponent.

Quiz

91.

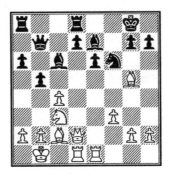

Karpov – Adams
Dos Hermanas 1993
White to move

Black would get counterplay from 21... bxc4 and ...♖dc8. Is there a better move than the routine 21 cxb5 ?

92.

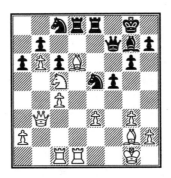

Bareev – Piket
Montecatini Terme 2000
White to move

Should White sacrifice with 24 ♘xb7 ♕xb7 25 ♗c7? What is the best alternative?

93.

Reti – Nimzovich
Berlin 1928
White to move

What should White do?

94.

Shirov – Gelfand
Monaco 2000
White to move

What should White do?

95.

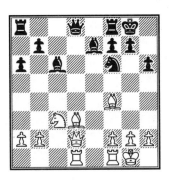

Kamsky – Lautier
Dortmund 1993
White to move

Is there a better move than the principled 16 ♖fe1 ?

96.

Aronian – Solak
Internet 2020
White to move

Black is preparing ...h4. Should White thwart him with 23 ♘ef4 or try something else?

97.

Aronian – Grischuk
St. Louis 2018
White to move

Black is ready to blockade with …f5 or …♗f5. Should White allow this or try 18 ♖xf7 ?

98.

Barlov – Benjamin
New York 1987
Black to move

What should Black do?

Chapter Nine:
Finishing Up

When you reach the end of the checklist, you are almost ready to make a move on the board. Almost.

Before you play it, there is one final task to perform. It may sound strange: You should look for a good reason *not* to play that move.

Like a scientist verifying his hypothesis, you want to be certain you are right. You can start by asking, "Is there a better move?"

When you spot a strong move, this is good news. You may be winning. There is a strong temptation to stop looking. But in favorable positions, particularly tactical positions, there are likely to be strong moves and stronger ones.

Carlsen – Korobov
Internet 2020
Black to move

There's a lot going on in this position, including the potential pawn push c5-c6-c7. Experienced players will recognize a mating pattern.

It should not be hard to see that White threatens 33 ♘f7+ ♚g8 34 ♘xd8+. But if you have learned your tactical patterns, you know 34 ♘h6+! ♚h8 would allow a smothered mate: 35 ♕g8+! ♖xg8 36 ♘f7.

Black's only alternative to resigning was **32...♖f8**, so he'd have 33 ♘f7+ ♖xf7.

Then, if you think about the position from White's perspective you would see 34 ♕xf7 as well as 34 ♕xa8+. You might mentally chalk up the point, play 33 ♘f7+ quickly and start thinking about your next game.

This is a mistake. You should look further for two reasons. The first is that Black might have a forcing reply to 34 ♕xf7 or 34 ♕xa8+.

He does: 34...♖f8! would turn the tables (34 ♕xf7 ♖f8 36 ♕-moves ♕xf2 mate).

This is discouraging, if not shocking news. But the ♘f7+ idea is so appealing that before you abandon it, you should try to make it work.

Then you could find 34 ♖d2!. With this move, f2 is protected (34...♕c3 35 ♕xa8+ and wins).

Magnus Carlsen likely saw all this before Black played 32...♖f8. Yet he instantly replied **33 ♖d2!**.

Black to move

This is the second reason to analyze further after 32...♖f8.

Carlsen's move wins faster than 33 ♘f7+, in view of 33...♕a3 34 ♘f7+ ♖xf7 35 ♕xa8+ ♖f8 36 ♖d8.

Black replied **33...♕c3** and lost after **34 e6 b3 35 e7**.

"When you see a good move, look for a better move" may be the oldest chess advice. It dates from the 10th century, before the modern rules of the game were formed. The pieces can move differently today, and there are time controls no one imagined then. This advice remains absolutely vital.

How Much Better Is Best?

Another old saying is, "Good is the enemy of best." But when your clock is ticking, there is a practical question: How much better is "best"?

In other words, is it worth analyzing a position once you have found a move you know is good? Is "good" good enough?

In the last example, the difference between the good 34 ♘f7+/35 ♖d2 and the better 34 ♖d2 was about +4.00, in computer terms. This is a lot, and it made finding 34 ♖d2! worthwhile.

One move later, after 34...♛c3, White could have searched for an alternative to 35 e6.

White to move

There is one. After 35 ♘b5! Black's queen is trapped.

The key continuation is 35...♛g3 36 ♕xa8!, so that 36...♖xa8 37 fxg3.

This is undeniably superior to the move Carlsen played, 35 e6. But this time the difference between good and best was slight. Sticking with 35 e6, when short of time, was wise.

Tweaked Tactics

The most likely way to turn a good move into a better one is to tweak the tactics. This is what 33 ♖d2! did in the last example. Here is another.

Bannik – Korchnoi
Kiev 1954
White to move

Is there a strong tactical idea available to White? Yes, in fact, there is another pattern based on a few pieces: White can sacrifice a rook on h7, followed by ♕xf7+.

214

Black's king would be forced to the h-file. This pattern has been used many times, and the king is often mated. Here this would be the case after 20 ♖h7+ ♚xh7 21 ♕xf7+ ♚h8 22 ♖h1+.

But in this version of the pattern, Black's king can avoid 21...♚h8?? and escape with 21...♚h6!.

White would run out of checks after 22 ♖h1+ ♚g5. He might even lose after 23 f4+?? ♕xf4+.

Once again, we have an appealing idea that just doesn't work – yet. Before abandoning it, White should try to improve on the variations he calculated.

Where should he start? Should he look for a win after 21...♚h6?

White to move

He can investigate 22 ♗d3 because it threatens ♕xg6 mate.

But he would give up on this move after seeing 22...♕g2!.

He could press on. Instead of 22 ♗d3, he can try inserting 22 ♖h1+ ♚g5 before 23 ♗d3.

However, 23...♖g8! is unclear. Disappointed by this, White can grasp at straws. Would 23 ♚b1 work? Then 24 f4+ ♕xf4 is not check – and 25 ♖g1+! wins.

The best way to try to tweak a tactical idea is often at the beginning of a calculated scenario, not at the end.

Going back to the first diagram White saw **20 ♖h2!**.

Black to move

By driving the queen back, the combination works. White would mate after 20...♕b6? 21 ♖h7+! ♔xh7 22 ♕xf7+ ♔h6 23 ♖h1+ ♔g5 24 f4. (Also good is 20 ♖df1, with the same idea).

Black was able to avoid mate with **20...♕c5** and then **21 ♖h7+! ♔xh7 22 ♕xf7+ ♔h6 23 ♖h1+ ♕h5**.

Material was nearly equal after **24 ♕f4+ ♔g7 25 ♖xh5 gxh5**, but White had a winning initiative after **26 ♕g5+ ♔f7 27 ♕xh5+ ♔e6 28 ♕g4+ ♔f6 29 ♗c4**.

Forcing Tweak

Even when a position is tactically quiet, a good idea can be enhanced by a forcing move.

Carlsen – Xiong
Internet 2020
White to move

What is Black's weakest point?

The answer seems to be the c6-pawn. Its best defender, the b5-bishop, can be driven away by a2-a4.

This suggests 25 ♖a1 and 26 a4. After the bishop moves, White would carry out his idea with ♖ac1 and ♖xc6.

216

But 25 ♖a1 has a drawback. After 25...♖ab8! and 26 a4 ♗d3, White's b2-pawn would be as weak as the c6-pawn.

So, let's turn to Black's second weak point, the e6-pawn. It can be targeted by a rook or by f2-f4-f5.

However, Black can meet 25 f4 with 25...♗a4! and be close to equal.

Should White hunt for a third weakness to pressure? Or should he turn to principled moves such as 25 f3 and ♔f2?

No, Carlsen blended the first two ideas with **25 ♖e1!**.

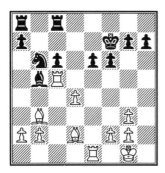

Black to move

Black has two ways of stopping ♗xe6+. Both have drawbacks.

The centralizing 25...♘d5 gives up the option of ...♗a4.

This means White is free to shoot for f2-f4-f5 – for instance, with 26 f4 ♖e8 27 f5.

If instead 26...♗d3, White would be making progress with 27 g4 f5 28 gxf5 ♗xf5 29 ♗d1 and 30 g4, for example.

Black chose **25...♖e8**. This left the c6-pawn underprotected.

Carlsen exploited it with **26 ♖a1!**.

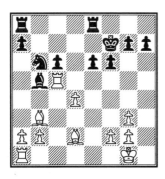

Black to move

217

The threat is once again 27 a4 ♗-moves 28 ♖xc6.

Black did not like 26...♗a4 27 ♗xa4 ♘xa4, apparently because of 28 ♖xc6 ♘xb2 29 ♖b1! ♘a4 30 ♖b7+. But this was his best chance.

He chose **26...♖ed8** instead.

This prompted Carlsen to calculate 27 a4 ♖xd4. He determined 28 axb5 ♖xd2 29 ♖xc6 would be convincing.

So, after **27 a4!**, Black chose **27... ♗c4**. He resigned after **28 ♗xc4 ♖xd4 29 a5 ♖xc4 30 axb6!**.

Endgames are much more tactical than many amateurs appreciate, because the tactics often involve a minor, almost trivial finesse. Here tweaking the ♖a1/a2-a4 idea with 25 ♖e1! was crucial.

Psychological Pitfall

You may have fallen into a trap of your own making:

You study a position and are attracted by Candidate Move A. But when you calculate its consequences, you are disappointed. You think your position deserves more.

So, you turn to Move B. It has merits. But when you analyze it you aren't impressed.

You become frustrated, particularly because you realize you have wasted time analyzing a move – or two – you won't play. Eventually you make a decision. Instead of a relatively good move A or move B, you end up playing C, a bad move.

Aron Nimzovich gave us a look inside his mind when he fell into this trap. This happened when he seemed to be thinking well, in the tournament that was his greatest triumph.

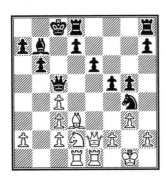

Yates – Nimzovich
Carlsbad 1929
White to move

218

Black has several positional assets, and they coalesce into a strong tactical idea: He can try to exploit the a8-h1 diagonal with the threat of 20...♕c6.

Then 21 ♗e4 fxe4 22 ♕xg4 would be answered by 22...e3!.

White can block the fatal diagonal with 21 f3. But then 21...h5! and 22...h4! would be decisive.

White anticipated this with **20 ♗e4!**.

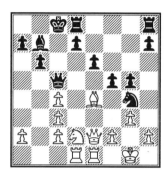

Black to move

Nimzovich admitted in his notes he was "rattled" by this. When he looked for a simple refutation, he found 20...fxe4 21 ♕xg4 was not the easy win he expected. He would be worse after 21...♕c6? 22 ♘xe4.

So, he turned to his other ways of replying to 20 ♗e4. Both 20...h5 and 20...♘f6 looked reasonable.

But when he calculated them, he was again disappointed by what he saw. In the end, he chose **20...♗a6**.

He was soon worse, **21 ♗g2 ♔c7 22 h3**, and eventually lost.

You can blame this on bad moves, 20...♗a6? and 21...♔c7?. But the real reason was he made three basic errors of thinking.

The first was giving up on the first candidate he looked at, 20...fxe4!. Then 21 ♕xg4 could be met by 21...h5! 22 ♕e2 h4.

He apparently missed the trick 23 ♘xe4 hxg3!, when Black wins. White would be sentenced to a bad endgame instead, after 23 ♕e3 ♕xe3 24 ♖xe3 d5.

Nimzovich's second thinking error was giving up on another good candidate, 20...h5.

219

He saw his dream of mate on g2 or h1 would be over after 21 &xb7+ &xb7. If he had looked further, he might have seen how 22 ©b3 ♛c7 and ...h4! would grant him good winning chances.

But the fundamental mistake Nimzovich made was assuming he was winning in the game's first diagram. After 20 &e4, he was merely better than White.

Checking The Final Box

Most games played below the master level are not won. They are lost. They are decided by bad moves, not good ones. This leads to the final checklist question: How might my move be a blunder?

It's a strange question. If you have been considering a particular candidate since you began going through the checklist, how could you have failed to detect a gross failing?

The answer is that the move selection process is so complex, you can be overwhelmed by sophisticated criteria concerning pawn structure, prophylaxis and the like. As a result, you can overlook something elementary.

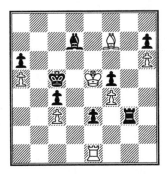

Kramnik – Ding Liren
Internet 2020
Black to move

The endgame is roughly balanced. Black can pick off the h6-pawn after ...♖h3.

But White, former World Champion Vladimir Kramnik, knew he was in no danger. He can win the f5-pawn after &e6. Or, if allowed, he can grab the h7-pawn after &g8.

So when Black played **51...♖h3**, Kramnik had a choice and 20 seconds on his clock to make it.

He could see how 52 ♗e6 would lead to a roughly even rook endgame after 52...♗xe6 53 ♔xe6 ♖xh6+ 54 ♔xf5.

He must have also seen that 52 ♗g8 ♖xh6 was harmless because of 53 ♖xe3.

Yet he chose **52 ♖xe3??** and resigned after **52...♖xe3+**.

"Of course," you might say. "It was time pressure. White only had 20 seconds left when he blundered."

But this does not explain disasters like this:

Nielsen – Karjakin
Wijk aan Zee 2005
White to move

The position hadn't changed significantly in more than 20 moves of maneuvering. White played **100 ♘b3**.

Black had about an hour left. He replied **100...♔g5??**.

Neither player realized at first what was wrong. Then White found **101 ♘xa1!**, and Black resigned.

You can explain this blunder, too. It wasn't due to a lack of time to think, but pure mental fatigue.

Yes, this also happens. But this doesn't explain a curious phenomenon of blunders: Good players may see they are making a horrible move almost at the same time they are making it.

Alburt – Wilder, US Championship 1986

1 d4 ♘f6 2 c4 g6 3 ♘c3 ♗g7 4 e4 d6 5 ♗e2 0-0 6 ♗g5 c5 7 d5 h6 8 ♗f4 b5 9 cxb5 a6 10 a4 g5 11 ♗e3 ♕a5 12 ♗d2 ♕b4 13 f3 ♘h5 14 ♕c2

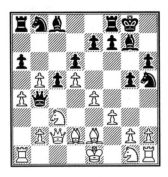

Black to move

Black thought he was following his carefully prepared moves. He played **14...axb5**.

"About a second later I heard myself say 'Uh-oh,'" he recalled.

Instead of 15 ♘xb5 ♕xb2, his opponent played **15 ♘d1!**. Black could resign on the spot. His queen is trapped.

This was not a speed game. Black, a grandmaster, had more than two hours on his clock when he played 14...axb5??.

Blunder Checking

Good blunder-checking begins with visualizing what the position will look like immediately after your intended move. This is a worthwhile habit even if you have to whisper to yourself "If I go there..."

Akopian – Meier
Istanbul 2012
Black to move

Spectators recalled how Black thought for some time here. He might hold a draw after 44...♕d7 45 ♕xe4+ ♔f6.

He played **44...exf3,** pressed his clock – and froze.

He resigned before White could win his queen with 45 ♕g4+!.

He could have avoided this by pausing, even for a few seconds, to picture in his mind what the board would look like after 44...exf3.

Envisioning

It is often easy to overlook a new tactical idea, such as the clearing of White's fourth rank by 44...exf3??. But even if you are aware of the tactical themes in a position, you can forget about them as your hand reaches for a piece.

Caruana – Giri
Internet 2020
White to move

If there were a caption under this diagram that read "Black to move and win," good players would quickly spot 26...♖xa4! (27 bxa4 ♖b1 mate).

Of course, Fabiano Caruana could see the threat and knew he should move his knight. He could have put up resistance by repositioning it, at c3 or at c4, after 26 ♘b2.

He preferred **26 ♘c5**. His knight can hop to a6 if attacked by a rook.

If he had envisioned this position more intently before he touched the knight, he would have seen the same tactic he was trying to avoid.

He resigned after **26...♖c4+!**, in view of 27 bxc4 ♖b1 mate.

Forgotten Information

Picturing what your move looks like can protect you from forgetting an opponent's tactical idea, as in the last example. It may also remind you of your defensive resources. Even if you were aware of them last move, you may forget them when making your next move.

Vachier-Lagrave – Caruana
Internet 2020
White to move

Black has just captured on d5. He is taking aim at the d3-pawn, with
...♖fd8 to come.

White replied **18 ♕c3**. When Black asks "What does he want?" he can
see White may dissolve his weakness with 19 d4!.

This would favor White after 19...exd4 20 ♘xd4 or 19...e4 20 ♘d2.

Before playing 18 ♕c3, he must have looked at the forcing reply
18...♖c5.

The only way to save his queen would be 19 ♕d2.

Black's rook would be misplaced on c5. It would be vulnerable to 20 b4!,
e.g. 20...axb4 21 axb4 ♖b5?, when 22 d4! threatens ♗xb5.

Black avoided all this with the practical **18...♖fd8!**. Once again, a
principled move made sense when complications (of 18...♖c5) were
unclear.

White to move

White answered by adding protection for that pawn, **19 ♖d2**. This was a
failure of memory as well as a failure to envision.

If he had remembered what he saw a move earlier – the possibility of 18...♖c5 19 ♕d2 – White would have realized in time that his move was a blunder.

He resigned after **19...♖c5!**.

Of course, it is annoying to have to do this visualizing routine before every move. But White's sense of danger should have alerted him when he looked at 18 ♕c3 ♖c5. It should have planted in his mind the significant news: "Be careful. Your queen has few squares."

Yesterday's Truth

Failing to appreciate new information is bad. So is relying on out-of-date information.

Suppose it is your opponent's move. While he is thinking, you notice you have a tactical idea you might use in reply. But before you can play it, your opponent moves and your tactic no longer works.

You subconsciously file your idea in the back of your mind. This is usually good. But it can quickly become yesterday's truth.

Caruana – Nakamura
Internet 2020
White to move

White instantly saw a good tactical idea, a discovered check on the b1-h7 diagonal. He only took seconds to set it up with **45 ♕d3**.

Computers regard the best way for Black to avoid the deadly ♘g5+ or ♘f6+ is to block the diagonal with 45...g6!.

But humans tend to dislike a loosening move like this. Black chose **45...♕g6** instead.

It was up to White to find a new tactical idea. He didn't disappoint his fans watching on-line.

White to move

He found **46 ♖c8!**. He had spotted the clever threat of 47 ♖xc6!. Then 47...♕xc6 48 ♘f6+ and 49 ♕h7 is mate.

Black had no way to defend the c6-pawn with other pieces (46...♖a6?? 47 ♕xa6).

He had to skate past other tactics, such as 46...♘f6?? 47 ♘xf6+! and wins (47...♗xf6 48 ♖h8+! ♔xh8 49 ♕xg6).

Black found the only move to guard the mating square, h7. He played **46...♘f8**.

White to move

Now White has a wide choice of quiet moves. The best of them eliminate Black tactics. For example, 47 f3 protects White's knight so his queen is freed to try ♕b3-b8.

Instead, he instantly played **47 ♖xc6**.

Of course, he saw Black could capture the rook. After all, he had calculated ♖xc6/...♕xc6 when he chose 46 ♖c8!.

But this was old information – one move old. He didn't ask himself what he would do now after **47...♛xc6!**.

He searched for a powerful discovered check. There was none, and he soon resigned.

Once again, a pause to visualize his move would reveal that 47 ♖xc6 deserved two question marks and not a game-winning exclamation point.

What To Remember

There are two ways you can trip when taking the final steps in selecting a move. The first is failing to look for a better move. Favorable positions often have good moves and superior ones. The difference between good and best can be trivial but it can also be huge.

The much greater mistake is the simplest chess mistake of all. It is failing to visualize what the move you want to play will look like once you make it.

Quiz

99.

Caruana – Nepomniachtchi
Internet 2020
White to move

White can win two pawns with 35 ♛xh6+! ♚xh6 36 ♘xf7+. Should he stop calculating and play this?

100.

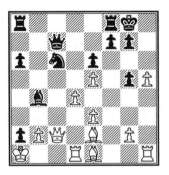

Wojtaszek – Harikrishna
Biel 2020
Black to move

After **25...♗xe1**, is there a better move than the routine 26 ♖dxe1?

101.

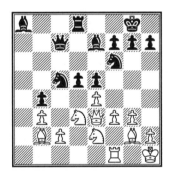

Wade – Petrosian
Saltsjöbaden 1952
Black to move

Is 21...♘xd3 the way to go?

102.

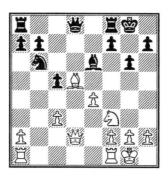

Giri – Carlsen
Internet 2020
White to move

The position seems to call for **15 ♗xe6**. Is this correct?

103.

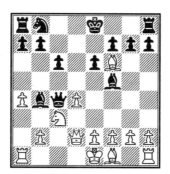

Alekhine – Euwe
World Championship match 1937
Black to move

White won after **10...gxf6 11 e4**. What did the players and dozens of annotators overlook?

104.

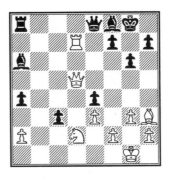

Svidler – Anand
Internet 2020
White to move

Can White do better than 35 ♘xe4?

105.

Geller – Szabó
Saltsjöbaden 1952
Black to move

Play went **31...♗c3 32 ♖e6**, threatening ♖g6. What were the mistakes?

106.

Anand – Leko
Internet 2020
Black to move

Compare 55...♛c2 and 55...♛d8.

107.

Korchnoi – Züger
Lenzerheide 2010
White to move

Did Black blunder by allowing **23 ♛xb4** ?

108.

Carlsen – Ivanchuk
Internet 2020
White to move

White wants to win with ♖f7 after a queen move. Evaluate 74 ♕e8, 74 ♕e6 and 74 ♕b3.

109.

Emanuel Lasker – Marshall
World Championship match 1907
Black to move

Black played **11...♗xh2+**, counting on **12 ♔xh2 ♕c7+** and **13...♕xc4**.

What was wrong with this?

110.

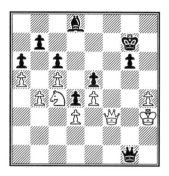

Leko – Anand
Internet 2020
Black to move

Black had been forcing matters for nearly 20 moves. He thought
65...♗xh4 was a winning breakthrough. Is it?

111. Szabó – Keres, Candidates tournament 1953

1 d4 d5 2 ♘f3 ♘f6 3 c4 dxc4 4 ♘c3 a6

White to move

White, an expert on the Black side of the Queen's Gambit Accepted, was
familiar with 4 ♕a4+ ♘bd7 5 ♘c3 a6. He chose **5 ♕a4+**, so 5...♘bd7
transposes.

Of course, 5...b5 is bad because of 6 ♘xb5 axb5 7 ♕xa8, right?

Quiz Answers

1. He overlooked the threat, **59 d6+!**. Then 59...♔e8 60 ♖h8 is mate or 59...♔f8 60 ♖g6! and ♖g8. Also 59...♔d8 60 ♖h8+ ♗e8 61 ♗b5. Instead of 58...♖xf2?, Black might have drawn with 58...♗e8 59 d6+ ♔d8.

2. Stop his threat of ...♘f4+ with a king move. Black resigned after **24 ♔g3!** rather than play out 24...♘e4+ 25 ♕xe4 ♕xc4.

3. The main threat was not 46 ♘xf5 but **46 ♘c6!** and 47 ♘xa5 or 47 d8(♕) wins.

4. White saw 19...♖xd4 and would have been safe after 19 ♘xf5. But he overlooked the second threat and lost after **19 ♘ce2? ♘xe5!** (20 dxe5? ♖xh4 mate).

5. Yes, he missed the greater threat of ...h5. He resigned after **40...exd4** in view of 41 ♕d2 h5! or 41 ♕xd4 h5! 42 ♘e3 ♕xf2+. Instead, 40 ♕c2 might have held.

6. Black threatened 33...g5!. White might survive after 33 ♖a4! g5 34 ♘f3 e4 35 ♘d2 ♕f6 36 ♘xe4 ♘xe4 37 ♖axe4!.

He lost after **33 ♘f3 ♕f6 34 ♕d2 e4** because his intended 35 ♘g5 would lose to 35...e3! (36 ♖xe3 ♕xg5). He resigned after **35 ♘h4 g5 36 ♗h3 gxh4 37 ♗e6 ♘d4 38 ♗xf7+ ♖xf7**.

7. 36 ♖a3! sets the table for a fork (36...♖xa3 37 ♕xc5 and 38 ♕xa3, or 38 ♕f8 mate). Black resigned after **36...♘xd3 37 ♕h4** because both the mating 38 ♕d8+ and 38 ♖xa3 were threatened.

8. It would be safe after 12...♗d7 13 a4 or 12...♘c7? 13 ♗xc7. But the knight was shown to be underprotected by **12...g5! 13 ♗xg5 ♘c7 14 a4 a6**. Or 13 ♗e5 g4.

9. After **38...♕c1!** the d2-knight and f1-bishop are underprotected (39 ♘f3 ♕xf1 mate). White resigned after 39 ♕b8+ ♔h7 40 ♕f4?? ♗xd2.

10. The overworked queen is distracted by **27 c4!**. Black resigned soon after **27...♕a4 28 b3! ♕a1+ 29 ♗f1 ♕e1 30 ♗e3**.

11. The bishop is vulnerable after **16...♖b4!**, followed by 17...♘xg4 (18 ♗xg7 ♕b6+ and ...♘e3) or 17...♖xd4. Black had a winning initiative after **17 a3 ♖xd4! 18 ♕xd4 ♘xg4 19 ♕xa7? e5!**. White would also be worse after 19 ♕c5 ♕d6.

234

12. No, the knight is still trapped after **13 b4! cxb4 14 ♘a4** and **15 ♗b6** or **15 ♘b6**. For example, 14...♘c8 15 ♘b6! ♘xb6 16 ♗xb6.

13. It put the queen on a pinning diagonal after **30 ♘xg6!**, e.g. 30...fxg6 31 ♕xa8! ♖xa8 32 ♗xd5, with a won endgame.

14. 22 ♗a3!, so that 22...♖fc8 23 ♘g3 ♕f7 24 ♘g5 ♕e8 25 ♘f7! wins. Similar is 22 ♘g3! ♕f7 23 ♗a3!. The game ended with **22...♖f7? 23 g4! ♕e4 24 ♘g5 resigns** (or 23...♕f4 24 ♗c1).

15. 29...b4! threatens the queen (30...♖b5). White resigned after **30 a4 ♖b6 31 ♘d4 ♗xd4 32 ♖xd4 ♘e2+**.

16. His rook was trapped after **52 ♖f3!** because of the threat of 53 ♖xf6! ♔xf6 54 ♕b2+.

17. No, **26...♕b4** attacked three unprotected pieces and won. No better was 26 ♘f6 ♕c5+! and mates. White would have had survival chances after 26 ♘fd2!.

18. The Black rook is underprotected after **23 ♖c8+ ♖d8 24 b4!** (24...♕xb4 25 ♖xd8+). Black resigned soon after **24...♕b6 25 ♗c7! ♖xc8 26 ♗xb6**.

19. He exposed the unprotected g7-bishop with **14 ♘f5! gxf5 15 ♗f4**, e.g. 15...♕e7 16 ♗xd6 f4 17 ♕xg7. Also good is 14 ♘e6!, so that 14...fxe6 15 ♗f4.

20. 23 ♘xb6! forced **23...♕xb6 24 ♖c8+ ♖d8** because 24...♔h7 25 ♕f5+ g6 26 ♕f6 is worse. Then **25 a5!** showed that Black's queen was overworked. He resigned soon after **25...♖xc8 26 axb6**.

21. 27 ♗a5! ♕a7 28 ♕c1! threatened the unprotected c6-bishop with 29 ♘xe6, as well as the underprotected h6-knight with 29 ♗d2! and ♗xh6. Black resigned after **28...e5 29 ♗d2 exd4 30 ♘d3**.

22. His best tactical ideas were the vulnerability of g3 and the a3-rook. He should attack both with 26...♕d6!. Then 27 ♘b1? ♕c5+ (28 ♔h1 ♗xd5+ or 28 ♔f1 ♖f7+).

23. White resigned after **24...♖xa4!** because the a1-rook is overworked (25 ♖xa4 ♗h3! 26 ♗xh3 ♕xf3+ 27 ♗g2 ♕d1+ and mates). Also lost is 27 ♔g1 ♗xc3 because ...♗xb4 as well as ...♗d4 mate is threatened.

24. 20 ♖f2?? created a mating pattern, 20...♕xh2+! 21 ♔xh2? ♘g3+ and mate next.

25. 30 ♕xg7+! ♔xg7 31 ♘xd7+ regained the queen with interest, 31...♔g8 32 ♘f6+ ♔f7 33 ♘d5+ and ♘xc7.

26. 33...♕e4! threatened 34...♗xf2+ (35 ♔xf2 ♖d2+) as well as 34...♖d5. The rest: **34 ♖b2 ♖d5 35 ♖e2 ♕b1+ 36 ♔h2 f6 White resigns**.

27. 16 e5! exploited the opened diagonal and threatened 17 b4!. Black would be lost after 16...g5 17 ♗d2 ♘dxe5 18 ♕e2 and f2-f4. He did not have enough compensation for the Exchange after **16....♘cxe5 17 ♗xe5 ♘xe5 18 ♗xa8 ♖xa8 19 ♕e2** and ♘d2.

28. 13 ♗g5! threatened ♗xf6, e.g. 13...fxg5 14 ♕e5+ ♔f7 15 ♘h6+ ♔f8 16 ♕xh8+. White won after **13...♖f8 14 ♕e5+! ♔f7** (14...fxe5 15 ♘d6 mate) **15 ♘d6+ ♔g7 16 ♘xb7**.

29. 23 ♗h4! seizes the abandoned diagonal, e.g. 23...f6 24 b4! ♘c6 25 ♕c4! or 24...♘b7 25 ♘d4. White won after **23...♕e8 24 ♘g5! h6 25 ♘h7!**. Or 24...g6 25 ♘xh7! ♔xh7 27 ♗f6! ♔g8 28 ♕e3 and ♕h6.

30. After **28 ♕c1!**, there was no defense to ♕h6 and mate (28...♔h8 29 ♕h6 ♖g8 30 ♘g5).

31. 4...e5! wins after 5 cxd5 cxd4 or 5 dxe5 d4. White was worse after **5 ♘xd5 cxd4 6 ♗d2 ♘f6** and lost after **7 ♗g5? ♘xd5! 8 ♗xd8 ♗b4+**.

32. White won after **33 ♖xe5!** because the f8-rook would hang after 33...dxe5. The safe way to prepare ...g3 was 32...♖g8 and 33...h4.

33. 29...♕c7! and ...♗d6, e .g. 30 ♕g4 ♗c5 31 e4 ♗d6, with a threat of 32...f5. White lost after **30 f4 ♗c5! 31 ♕c3 gxf4**. Also 31 ♕e4 ♗xe3! 32 ♕xe3 gxf4.

34. 25 ♗d5! prompted resignation (25...♖xd5 26 ♕c8+).

35. White had a greater threat than ...♗xf1, **18 ♘d4!** and 19 ♘dxe6!. Black saw how bad 18...♗d7 19 ♖d3 would be. He lost after **18...♗e8 19 ♘dxe6! fxe6 20 ♘xe6 ♕a7 21 e5 dxe5 22 ♘xf8**.

36. He allowed **45...g5!** to create a winning passed pawn. White resigned in view of 46 hxg5 h5! or 46 fxg5 h5!, followed by ...♔xh4-g4 and ...h4-h3.

37. White resigned after **29...e2!** because of 30 ♕xe2 ♘f3+ 31 ♕xf3 ♖xe1+ 32 ♔f2 ♖f1+!.

38. He allowed **36...♘c5!** and ...♘d3, in view of 37 dxc5 ♗xc5+ 38 ♘e3 ♖xe3! 39 ♗xe3? ♗xe3+ 40 ♔xe3 ♕b6+ and ...♕xg1. Black won after **37 ♔g2 ♘d3 38 ♗g3 ♗d6 39 ♗xd6 ♕xd6 40 gxf6 ♘e1+**.

39. No, **15 g4!** prepared to open the g-file and a2-g8 diagonal. Black was lost after **15...♗d7 16 c5! ♗xe5 17 dxe5 ♕e7 18 ♖g1 b6 19 ♗c3 g6 20 ♗c4!**.

40. With **19...♖g8!**, so that 20 ♗f3 ♖xe5 21 ♕xe5 ♗xf3 (or 20...♗d6). White resigned after **20 g3 ♗g7!** when he saw 21 f4 ♗xe5 22 fxe5 ♕c6!.

41. **56 ♕d2??** allowed 56... ♕xe4! (57 fxe4 ♖f1 mate).

42. White can recover after 10...♗f5 11 ♖e1 or 10...cxd4 11 a3. Best is the developing move **10...♖d8**, e.g. 11 ♗e3 cxd4 12 ♗xd4? ♗xf3. Black eventually won after **11 ♕b3 ♗xf3 12 gxf3 ♖xd4 13 ♗e3 ♖d3**.

43. **14...b6!**, based on 15 ♘xb6? ♖b8, allowed him to build a strong dark-square pawn formation, **15 ♘c3 c5 16 ♕a3 d4! 17 ♘ce2 a5!**, with advantage.

44. Black's last move left the e5-pawn underprotected and made **16 c5! bxc5 17 dxe5** positionally desirable.

Black could not afford 17...♗xe5 18 ♘xe5 ♕xe5 because of 19 ♗h7+ and ♖xe5. He resigned after **17...♖xe5 18 c4 ♖fe8 19 ♘xe5 ♗xe5 20 ♗xe5 ♖xe5 21 ♖ae1 ♖e6 22 ♕d2**.

45. Putting a rook on a good file, **19...♖bd8!**, was based on 20 ♖xe7 ♕d6! and 20 b5 ♕b6 21 ♗e3 ♗c5. White lost eventually after **20 ♗xb7? ♕c4 21 ♖xd8 ♖xd8 22 ♗e3 ♕xb4**.

46. No, **10 c5! ♗xb2 11 ♘d2** points out the hole at d6 that can be exploited by ♘c4. Then 11...♗xa1 12 ♕xa1 would threaten ♕xh8+. Instead, Black was much worse after **11...0-0 12 ♖b1 ♗g7 13 ♘c4**.

47. Weakening the kingside this way is good if White cooperates with 21 gxh5 ♘xh5, followed by ...♕c4 and ...♘g7-f5. But after **21 h3!**, Black was much worse: **21...a5 22 a3 ♖d7 23 ♖f3! ♕d8 24 ♖b1 ♗g5 25 ♖bf1 axb4 26 axb4 ♗e7**. He survived when White failed to find 27 gxh5 ♘xh5 28 ♖xf7! and wins.

48. "Passed pawns must be pushed" – **19 b5! ♗xc5 20 b6! ♗xd4 21 ♕xd4**.

Then 21...♘c6 22 ♕d3 ♘a6 23 ♘xd5 is bad. Black was losing after **21...♘cb5 22 ♘xb5 ♘xb5 23 ♗xb5 ♗xb5**, and now 24 b7 ♖b8 25 ♗a3.

49. There are two. One is 20...e5 (21 dxe5 ♘d7 and ...♘xe5). The other is **20...c5!**, so that 21 bxc5? ♗xf3 22 gxf3 ♖d5! and ...♖g5+ or ...♖h5. Or 21 ♗xb7 cxd4!. Instead, **21 dxc5 ♗xf3 22 gxf3 ♖xd2 23 ♕xd2 ♖d8** and ...♖d3 left White struggling to survive.

50. No, **11 e4!** seizes the key e4-square, based on 11...♘xe4 12 c4, winning material. For example, 12...♕f5 13 ♘g5. Or 12...♕c6 13 ♘e5 ♕d6 14 ♗xe4! ♕xd4 15 ♗xb7.

51. Principles call for …d5, so 14…♘c7! was better than 14…♖b8. Black would have more than a pawn's compensation after 15 ♗xb7 ♖b8 16 ♗f3 d5! 17 cxd5 ♘xd5.

After **16 ♖a3**, Black equalized with **16…d5! 17 ♘xd5 ♘xd5 18 cxd5 ♗xd5 19 ♖d3 ♗xf3** based on **20 ♖xd8 ♗xd1 21 ♖xb8** and now 21…♖xb8 22 ♔xd1 ♘d6.

52. 12 c5! frees the c4-square for a strong ♘c4. Play continued **12…dxc5 13 ♘c4 e5 14 f4** with the idea of fxe5 and ♗f4. Black resigned after **14…♗c6 15 fxe5 ♗xb5 16 exf6 ♗xc4 17 e5 a6 18 ♕g4 gxf6 19 ♕xc4 fxe5 20 ♖f1! f6 21 ♕e6+ ♔d8 22 ♖d1**.

53. White should not give up on **16 b5!** until he has looked for a good answer to 16…♗xa3. He would have more than enough compensation after 17 ♘e5! ♗d7 18 ♘a4 and ♘b6. Black declined the pawn, **16…♗d7 17 bxc6 bxc6**, and was steadily worse after **18 ♘a4 ♖ac8 19 ♘b6**.

54. 16 c4! so that 16…dxc4 17 d5! wins a piece (17…exd5 18 e6 is the fork). Black became desperate, **16…g5 17 hxg5 ♘xg5 18. ♘xg5 ♖dg8**, and resigned after **19 cxd5! exd5 20 e6 ♕e8** (20…♕d8 21 ♘f7) **21 ♘xd5 ♗d6 22 ♘xb6+**.

55. The unlikely **12 d4!** is based on 12…cxd4 13 ♘xd4! exd4 14 e5! and wins, with ♗xc6+ or exf6+. Black's best was **12…♘d7!**. He was worse after **13 dxe5 dxe5 14 ♘h6**.

56. He calculated **18 f5! ♘e7 19 ♗b3! ♘xf5** until he saw **20 ♗a4+!**. He had a decisive attack after **20… ♔e7 21 ♕d3 ♕b8 22 ♕d7+**.

57. The best idea is e3-e4-e5. The evolutionary method, 25 ♖de1, allows Black to stand well after 25…♗xd3! 26 ♗xd3 ♔g7 (27 e4? ♗xd4! 28 exd5 ♕b4!). The revolutionary way is **25 e4! dxe4 26 ♘f4**, based on 26…exf3? 27 ♗xf5. Black was worse after **26…♗g7 27 fxe4 ♗g4**, when 28 ♗b3! would have been strong (28…♗xd1 29 ♘xg6).

58. With **10 g4!** and 11 g5/♕c3 White aims at g7. Black sought counterplay against his best target, the b4-pawn, with **10…a5 11 g5 ♘d5**. But after **12 ♖g1 axb4 13 ♕d4!** he was nearly lost. He resigned soon after **13…f6 14 gxf6 ♕xf6? 15 ♖xg7+ ♔xg7 16 ♕g4+ ♔h8 17 ♗xf6+ ♖xf6 18 ♘g5**.

59. The h2-square. Black can exploit it with 28…♗f4 followed by 29…♗b8! and 30…♕d6. He preferred **28…♕d6 29 ♕b3 ♗d8!**. Then 30 ♘xd5 ♗xd5 31 ♗xd5 ♗c7! 32 f4 ♖e3 and 31 ♕xd5 ♕f4 would be bad. White resigned after **30 ♗g2? ♕f4 31 ♖c1 ♗c7 32 ♖fd1 ♖f6 33 ♕c2 ♖e3! 34 ♔f1 ♖xc3** (35 bxc3 ♗b5+).

60. The weakest White point is the c4-pawn. It can be attacked by the e6-bishop and a knight after **15...♘c8!** and ...♘b6. White sought counterplay against the d6-pawn with **16 ♖fd1**. But he would have been worse after 16...♕e7, e.g. 17 ♖ac1 ♘b6 18 ♘b1 a5. Or 17 ♘a4 a6 18 ♖d2 b5!.

61. 14 ♘g4! and 15 ♗g5 targets f6 and f7. For example, after 14...♘xg4 15 fxg4 ♗e6 16 ♘d5 or 15...♘e6 16 ♕f3. Black became desperate, **14...♗e6 15 ♗g5 ♘xg4 16 ♗xd8 ♘e3**, and lost after **17 ♕c1 ♗xc4 18 ♕xe3 ♘xc2 19 ♕d2 ♘xa1 20 ♗f6!**.

62. 15...♔d7! safeguards e6 so that **16...h5!** can take aim at the queen and king. White was in trouble after **16 ♗e2 h5! 17 fxe6+ fxe6 18 gxh5 g4** and hopeless following **19 ♕g2 ♖xc3 20 bxc3 ♗xe4 21 ♕f2 ♘xh5 22 ♗f4 g3!**.

63. Black can dream of targeting g2 with ...♖ad8-d6-g6. But the f-file is his Achilles heel after16 f3!, e.g. 16...f5 17 fxe4 fxe4 18 ♖f2 and 19 ♖af1. Play continued **16 f4 exf3?** (16...♕h4) **17 ♘xf3 ♕g3 18 ♖f2 ♖ad8 19 ♗c4**. Black found nothing better than **19...♘f6**, and eventually lost after **20 ♗xf6 gxf6 21 ♖af1**.

64. A case can be made for d6, after 26 ♖f2 and 27 ♖fd2. But Black cannot defend f6 after **26 ♕c3!**. Black stopped ♘g4 with **26...h5** but lost after **27 g4!**. No better is 26...e5 27 ♘d5 ♕d8 28 f5.

65. Around g3, after **26...h5!**. White was lost after **27 ♕c2? h4! 28 ♖c1 hxg3! 29 ♕xc6 gxh2+ 30 ♔g2 ♕xc6 31 ♖xc6 ♘xf2!**. Better but not good was 27 ♘c5 h4 28 ♗xe4 dxe4 29 ♕e3 ♕c8.

66. 26...♗a8! eyes mate on h1 after ...♕c6 or ...♕b7. For example, 27 ♗xd8 ♕xd8 28 ♕xe5 ♕b6+ 29 ♖e3 ♕b7 30 ♕e6+ ♖f7. Or 27 h4 ♕c6 28 ♔h2 ♕b6+! 28 ♗e3 ♕g6. White resigned after **27 ♕xb5? ♖b8** in view of 28 ♕e5 ♕b7 or 28 ♕c4+ ♕xc4 29 bxc4 ♖b2 and ...♖g2+.

67. He should target g7 with 35 c4! and ♗c3. He would be better after 35...bxc4 36 bxc4 ♗xc4 37 ♗c3 ♘f6 38 ♗xe4.

68. 13...g5! exploits a traffic jam of White pieces on the kingside, e.g. 14 ♗e3 g4! (15 ♘e1 ♘xe5). White went for **14 ♗g3 g4** (also good is 14... h5! 15 h3 h4 16 ♗h2 g4) **15 ♘xc6 ♗xc6 16 ♘e1**. Black's attack prevailed after **16...h5 17 f4** (17 ♗f4 ♗g5) **gxf3 18 ♘xf3 h4**.

69. Black is weak along the a1-h8 diagonal and **26 ♕b2!** pinned the f6-knight. White threatened 27 ♘h5+! gxh5 28 ♖g3+ and 29 ♕xf6(+) with a winning attack. Black had to play **26...♕e7**. But then **27 ♘d4!** set up a fork on f5. He conceded a pawn, **27...♔g8 28 ♘xc6 bxc6 29 ♖xc6**, and eventually lost.

70. White will win the d6-pawn, the weakest target, because 14...♔e7? allows 15 ♖xf6! and ♘d5+. However, **14...♗e6 15 ♕xd6 ♖c8** illustrates Bernstein's irony. The most important factors now are White's inferior pawn structure and bishop and his vulnerable queenside (...b5-b4 or ...♘d7-b6-c4). Black was soon equal, **16 a4 h5 17 h3 ♕xd6 18 ♖xd6 ♘d7 19 h4 ♔e7 20 ♖d2 ♘b6 21 ♘d5+ ♗xd5 22 exd5 ♘c4**, and went on to win.

71. Black wanted to play ...♗f3 or ...♘f3+. He was rewarded with **31 ♖xe8?? ♖xe8 32 ♕xe8 ♘f3+** and wins (33 ♗xf3 ♗d7+ or 33 ♔h1 ♕d3!). But **30...♘e8?** should have turned out badly after **31 ♔h1!** threatens ♖xe8. For example, 31...f5 32 ♖b6, with advantage.

72. **19 g4!** and **19...♘d6 20 c3 ♖e8 21 ♘g3** stopped counterplay. White won after **21...f6 22 ♕c2! h6 23 ♕d2 ♘d8? 24 ♗xh6! gxh6 25 ♘h5 ♖f8 26 ♕xh6 f5 27 ♕g6+ ♔h8 28 ♘f6 resigns**.

73. White can stop 17...b4! with **17 ♕g5!** and win by doubling rooks (18 ♖h4, 19 ♖dh1) or going for f3-f4-f5. Black was lost after **17...♕c7 18 e5 dxe5 19 ♗xe5 ♕c5 20 f4 ♖b7 21 ♗xg6!**.

74. After **13 ♔h1**, Black cannot meet f2-f4/e4-e5 because ...♘xe2 is not a check. He was losing after **13...g5 14 ♖c1 d6 15 f4 gxf4 16 ♘xf4 ♕g5 17 ♘h5** and ♘f6+.

75. He should anticipate ...♖fb8 with 20 a3 ♖fb8 (threat of ...♗xc5) 21 ♕d1!. Instead, he was losing after **20 0-0?? ♖fb8 21 ♖fc1 ♗xc5 22 ♕a4 ♗xd4 23 cxd4 ♖xb4**.

76. **23 f4!** stopped 23...♘e5 and prepared to win with 24 ♖ac1 and 25 ♕xc8. Now 23...♘f8 24 ♖ac1 ♗e6 25 ♗xe6 and 25...♕xe6 26 ♘c5 or 25...♘xe6 26 g4!. Instead, he lost after **23...♕g6 24 ♖ac1 ♘f8 25 ♕xc8 ♖xc8 26 ♖xc8 ♘6h7 27 ♖dd8**.

77. The direct way is 26 ♕h4 followed by ♘g4. Black can prolong the game with 26...♘c4 27 ♖xc4! bxc4 28 ♘g4 ♖g8. White preferred the prophylactic **26 b3!**, which rules out ...♘c4xe5. The game ended with **26...♖c3 27 ♘e2 ♖xc1 28 ♖xc1 ♗d6 29 ♖c8! resigns**.

78. 28 exf5? ♕xc2 was equal (29 f6? ♗c6!). But 28 ♖bc1! would have stopped ...♕xc2, so that exf5 wins. For example, 28...♖af8 29 exf5 ♗xf5 30 ♖xf5.

79. White wants to trade bishops, such as with 21 ♗xe4 ♕xe4 22 ♕xc6 or 21 ♕c4 ♗xg2+ 22 ♔xg2. Therefore **20...♗f5!**, so that 21 ♕xc6 ♖ac8 or 21 ♖xc6 ♖fd8 22 ♖c1 ♖ac8 wins. White might survive after 21 ♘g1 and 22 ♗f3 but lost after **21 ♘f4 ♗d2! 22 ♖xc6? ♖ab8 23 e3 ♗xe3!** (24 fxe3 ♕xe3).

80. Opening the a3-f8 diagonal invited **25 ♗c1!** and 26 ♗a3. White pieces soon dominated, **25...♗d7 26 ♗a3 bxc2 27 ♖c1 ♖fc8 28 ♖xc2 ♖a8 29 ♖ca2 ♗e8 30 ♗d6**. He won after **30...♖xa2 31 ♖xa2 ♕d7 32 ♕c1! ♗f7 33 ♕b1! ♕e8 34 ♕b7 ♔h7 35 ♖a6**.

81. The b5-pawn is the weakest and **28 ♗d1** and **29 ♗e2** is best. This would also threaten 29 g5 and 30 ♗g4!. Black resigned after **28...c6 29 dxc6 ♖xc6** (30...♗xc6 31 g5!) **30 ♕xb5**.

82. With **22 ♘b1!** she prepared ♘d2-c4xa5. After **22...♗f8 23 ♘d2 ♗c5 24 ♘dc4 ♗xb6 25 ♘xb6 ♔f8** her rooks penetrated, **26 ♖d2! ♔e7 27 ♖ad1 ♖f8 28 ♘xc8+ ♖fxc8 29 ♖d7+ ♔f6 30 ♗xe6 fxe6 31 g4!**. Black resigned before ♖1d3-f3+.

83. With **19...♗f5!** and ...♗e6. He was better after **20 ♘f3 ♗e6 21 ♖4c2 ♘d5** (or 21...♗d5), and he eventually won.

84. **23 a4!** and ♗a3. White gradually improved his position, **23...♖ab8 24 ♗a3 ♕d7 25 axb5 axb5 26 ♖a1**. He won the endgame after **26...♕xg4 27 hxg4 ♘c8 28 ♘f5**.

85. He should improve his knight. One way is 20...f6 21 exf6 ♘xf6 and ...♘e4. But **20...♘b8!** is better. For example, 21 0-0 ♘c6 22 ♕c5 ♕a5 23 ♕xb5 ♕c3 and ...♘b4. After **22 ♕d2 ♕b6+ 23 ♔h1 ♕a5 24 ♕xa5 ♖xa5** and ...♘b4 or ...♘d4 he had the upper hand.

86. **32 ♗f4!** adds a killing attacker with a threat of 33 ♗d6 and ♕h7 mate. After **32...♖a6 33 ♗e5! ♔f8**, White could have ended matters soon after 34 ♖de1!.

87. No, **41 ♖d3??** was only equal after **41...♖a1! 42 ♖xa1 ♕xd3**. He could have won with 41 ♕g7+ or 41 ♕h5+.

88. The attack would end after 18 g6 fxg6 19 ♕xg6 ♕f5+. Best was **18 ♘g1!** followed by ♘h3 or ♗xh5. Play continued **18...g6 19 ♘h3 ♕d6** (not 19...♕xh4 20 f4! followed by ♗d3 and f4-f5) **20 f4!**.

Black had no defense to the plan for f4-f5, ♖df1, ♗d3 and ♘f4. He lost after **20... a5 21 f5 ♖fe8 22 ♖df1 ♘f8 23 ♘f4 ♗d8 24 ♗d3 ♔g7 25 fxg6 fxg6 26 ♗xg6 ♘xg6 27 ♘xh5+**.

89. **44 ♗b5!** and ♗xc6. White won after **43...g6 44 ♗b5! cxb5 45 c6 ♔f6 46 ♖xd7 ♕f8 47 ♘e5!**, in view of 47...♖h7 48 c7 or 47...♘h6 47 ♖f7+! and ♘d7+.

90. More ambitious is **20...♖a7**, so the rook can defend h7 and counterattack on the f-file, e.g. 21 ♗d3 ♖f7 threatens 22...♗xg4! 23 fxg4 ♘e4+ and wins.

White was worse after **21 ♗g5 ♖f7 22 ♘h3 ♕e7!** and lost following **23 ♘f4 ♕e5 24 ♖b3? ♘h5! 25 gxh5 ♖xf4**.

91. Yes, **21 ♘d5!** based on 21...♘xd5? 22 cxd5 ♗xg5 23 dxc6! and wins. White had the upper hand after **21...♗xd5 22 cxd5 ♘xd5 23 ♗e4!** and won after **23...♗xg5 24 ♕xg5 ♕b6 25 ♗xd5 exd5 26 ♖e7**.

92. White's advantage all but disappeared after **24 ♘xb7? ♕xb7 25 ♗c7 ♖d7!**. But **24 ♗c7!** would have been strong, e.g. 24...♖xd1+ 25 ♖xd1 ♘xc4 26 ♘xb7 (26...♖xe3 27 ♖d8+ ♗f8 28 ♕b4).

93. Routine moves would turn a poor position to a bad one after, for example, 17 ♘f1 ♖e8 followed by ...♖b8, ...♕c7 and ...b4. But after **17 e4! dxe4 18 ♘xe4**, he could escape, e.g. 18...♘xe4? 19 ♘xe4 ♗xe4 20 ♗xc4!. White had good practical chances after **18...♗xe4 19 ♘xe4 ♘xe4 20 ♕c2 f5 21 ♗f3**.

94. Routine moves like 26 ♘c2 ♘c6 are little help. But **26 ♕a3! ♕xa3 27 bxa3** allowed White to improve relentlessly: **27...♖d8 28 ♖d3 b5 29 g3 ♖e4 30 ♔g2 b4 31 a4**, intending ♖c1-c7. He eventually won.

95. Black would be equal after 16 ♖fe1 ♗c5. But **16 ♗xh6! gxh6 17 ♕xh6** threatened 18 ♖fe1 and ♖e3-g3+ or 18 ♗c4 and ♖d3-g3+. Black resigned after **17...♖e8 18 ♗c4 ♗d7 19 ♖d4 ♗f8 20 ♕g6+ ♗g7 21 ♕xf7+ ♔h8 22 ♖h4+ ♘h7 23 ♖xh7+ ♔xh7 24 ♕h5+ ♗h6 25 ♗d3+ ♔g8 26 ♕xh6**.

96. Only equal is 23 ♘ef4 ♘xf4 24 ♕xf4 ♖g4 25 ♕d2 h4 26 ♘xh4? ♖xg3!. But **23 ♖xf5! exf5 24 ♘e3!** and ♘xf5 assured White of the upper hand. After some sloppy play, **24...♕g5 25 ♖xf5 ♕h6 26 ♕d3?** (26 ♘f4!) **h4? 27 ♘g4**, he prevailed, **27...♕h7 28 ♘f6 ♕h6 29 g4 ♖gh7 30 ♖h5 ♕g7 31 ♕f5+ ♔b8 32 ♘xh7** and so on.

97. **18 ♖xf7? ♔xf7 19 ♖f1+** works after 19...♔g8 20 ♗xe4 ♕xe4? 21 ♕xe4 ♖xe4 22 ♖f8 mate. But White was running out of bullets after **19...♗f5 20 g4 g6**, e.g. 21 ♕c1 ♖e6 22 ♕h6 ♔g8. He later won on a blunder.

98. His position would be critical after 22...♖fd8 23 ♕e2 d5, e.g. 24 exd5 exd5 25 ♘d4! with a killing threat of 26 ♘f5. Black went for **22...♘xf4! 23 gxf4 ♗xf4** and threatened 24...f5! 25 exf5 ♗e3+, followed by ...♖xf5. Chances would be nearly equal after 24 ♕d4! f5. Instead, White lost after **24 ♕e2? f5 25 e5 g5 26 ♗g2 g4 27 ♘h2? ♗xg2 28 ♕xg2 ♖xc4 29 ♖bd1 ♔h8 30 ♖xd7 ♖g8**.

99. No, **35 ♖e8!** is better, in view of 35...♘xe8 36 ♕xf7+ ♔h8 37 ♘xe8 ♕xd4 38 ♘f6. Or 35...♕xe8 36 ♘xe8+ ♘xe8 37 ♕b8 ♗d7 38 ♕d8.

100. No, 26 ♖dxe1 ♖fc8 27 ♖c1 would confer some advantage. But **26 h6?** was good for Black after **26...♖fc8!** (27 hxg7 ♗h4!). Or as the game continued, **27 ♖dxe1 ♘b4!**.

101. This move is good. Black is better after 22 cxd3 d4 22 ♕d2 ♕b6 or 22 ...dxe4 23 dxe4 ♘d7 24 ♖c1 ♕d6. But **21...♘cd7!** is best. It keeps the c2-pawn as a target and adds the e4-pawn as well. For example, 22 ♖c1 dxe4 23 fxe4 ♗c5! wins a pawn (24 ♘xc5 ♘xc5). White was lost after **22 exd5 ♕xc2 23 ♘ec1 ♘xd5 24 ♕f2 ♕xf2 25 ♖xf2** and now 25...♘e3!.

102. No, 15 ♕h6! would have won, e.g. 15...♗xd5 16 ♘g5 ♖e8 17 exd5 (17...♕xd5? 18 ♕xh7+ ♔f8 19 ♖fe1). White only drew after **15 ♗xe6?? ♕xd2 16 ♗xf7+ ♖xf7 17 ♘xd2 ♖d8**.

103. 10...♘b3! clearly favors Black, e.g. 10 ♗h4 ♘d7 and ...♘b6!. Or 10 ♗xg7 ♖g8 11 ♗e5 c5.

104. Yes, 35 ♖xf7! ♕xf7 36 ♗e6 may hold, e.g. 36...♖a7 37 ♗xf7+ ♖xf7 38 ♘xe4. Instead, **35 ♘xe4??** should have been punished by 35...c2! because of 36...c1(♕)+.

105. 32 ♖e8! would have threatened 33 ♗h7+ and reached a winning endgame of 32...♖xe8 33 ♕xe8+ ♕f8 34 ♕e6+. But **32 ♖e6??** lost to **32...b3!**, in view of 33 ♗xb3 ♕d4+ or 33 ♖g6 bxc2. Instead of 31...♗c3??, the position would be balanced after 31...♗d4+ 32 ♔h1 ♗f2! (33 ♖e8?? ♕a1+ or 33 ♖f1 g3).

106. **55...♕c2??** threatened to queen with discovered check. But it allowed mate after **56 ♖f8+ ♔g7 57 ♕f7+**. Black would have won quickly after 55...♕d8!.

107. No, this was a White blunder because **23...♕g6!** threatened mate as well as 24...cxb4.

108. 74 ♕e8! wins (74...♔h6 75 ♖f8). After 74 ♕e6? ♔h6, White should repeat the position, 75 ♕e3+ ♔h7, so that 76 ♕e8! is still available. Worst was **74 ♕b3?? ♕d7+!**, and Black won.

109. After **12 ♔xh2** Black realized 12...♕c7+ would be foiled by 13 ♘e5. He resigned soon after **12...h4.**

110. There was no follow-up to **66 ♔xh4.** Black resigned after **66...♕h2+ 67 ♔g4 ♕h5+ 68 ♔g3 ♕g5+ 69 ♔h3** because the checks are ending (69...♕h6+ 70 ♔g2 ♕g5+ 71 ♕g3).

111. No, **5...b5** 6 ♘xb5?? ♗d7 costs a piece. White had to play 6 ♕c2 and slowly lost. Black spent 15 minutes before playing 5...b5. If the move was as important as he thought, it was worthwhile taking time to make sure.

Other chess books available from Batsford

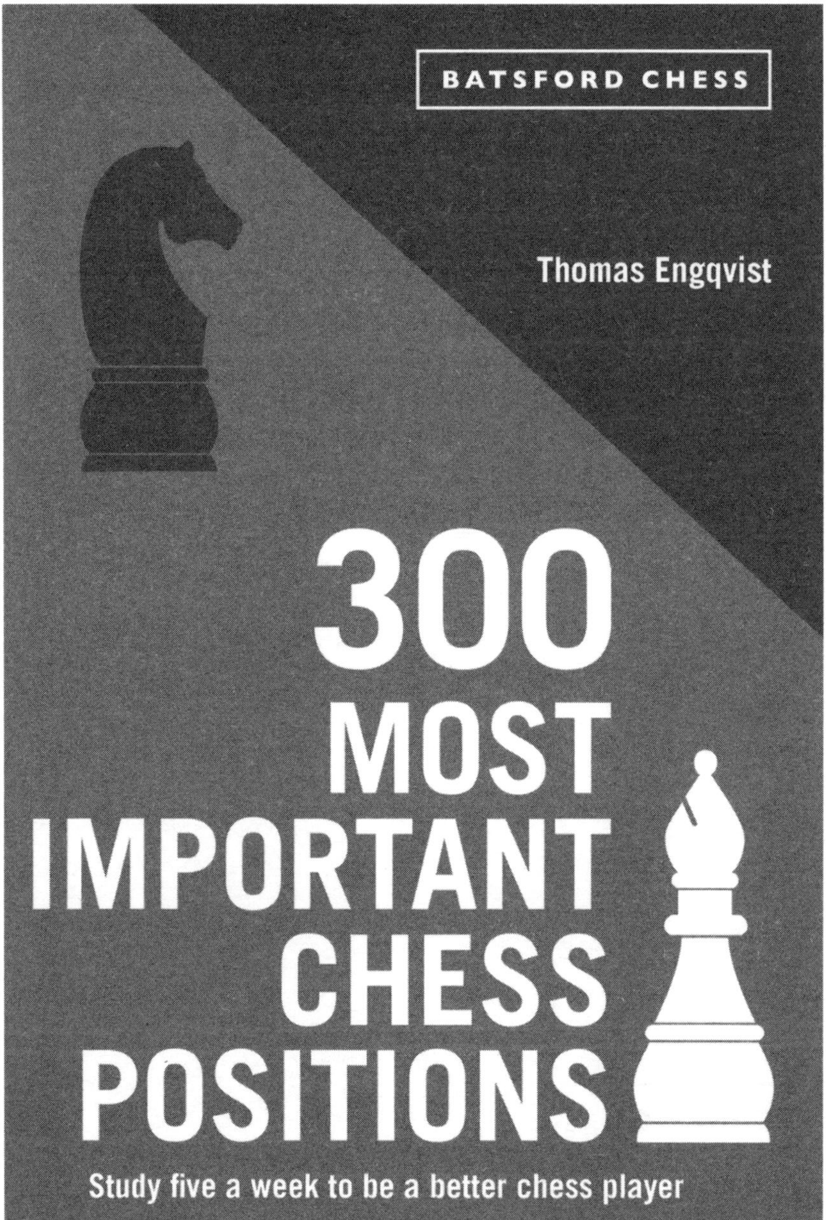

**300 MOST IMPORTANT
CHESS POSITIONS**
Thomas Engqvist
9781849945127 | £16.99 | PB
304 pages

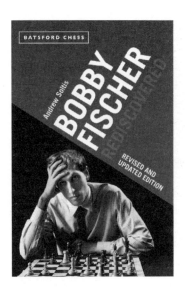

**BOBBY FISCHER
REDISCOVERED**
Andrew Soltis
9781849946063 | £16.99 | PB
312 pages

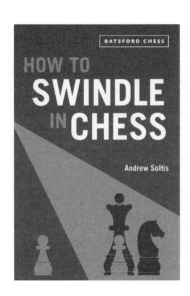

**HOW TO SWINDLE IN
CHESS**
Andrew Soltis
9781849945639 | £16.99 | PB
240 pages

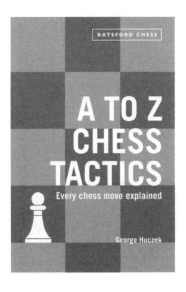

A TO Z CHESS TACTICS
George Huczek
9781849944465 | £17.99 | PB
352 pages

**365 CHESS
MASTER LESSONS**
Andrew Soltis
9781849944342 | £16.99 | PB
384 pages

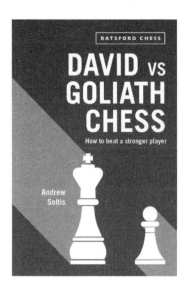

DAVID VS GOLIATH CHESS
Andrew Soltis
9781849943574 | £15.99 | PB
238 pages

WHAT IT TAKES TO BECOME A CHESS MASTER
Andrew Soltis
9781849940269 | £14.99 | PB
208 pages

PAWN STRUCTURE CHESS
Andrew Soltis
9781849940702 | £16.99 | PB
286 pages

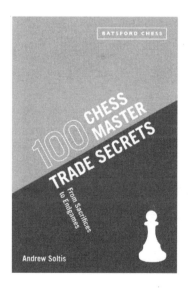

100 CHESS MASTER TRADE SECRETS
Andrew Soltis
9781849941082 | £14.99 | PB
208 pages

YOUR KINGDOM FOR MY HORSE: WHEN TO EXCHANGE IN CHESS
Andrew Soltis
9781849942775 | £15.99 | PB
208 pages

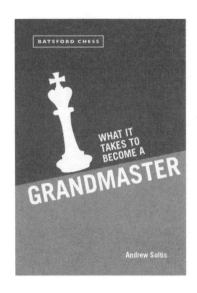

WHAT IT TAKES TO BECOME A GRANDMASTER
Andrew Soltis
9781849943390 | £15.99 | PB
320 pages

NEW ART OF DEFENCE IN CHESS
Andrew Soltis
9781849941600 | £15.99 | PB
288 pages

MY 60 MEMORABLE GAMES
Bobby Fischer
9781906388300 | £15.99 | PB
384 pages

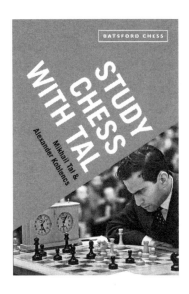

STUDY CHESS WITH TAL
Mikhail Tal, Alexander Koblencs
9781849941099 | £15.99 | PB
272 pages

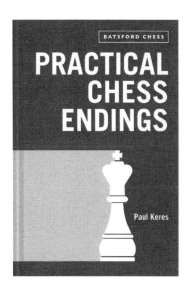

PRACTICAL CHESS ENDINGS
Paul Keres
9781849944953 | £16.99 | PB
352 pages

THE MOST INSTRUCTIVE GAMES OF CHESS
Irving Chernev
9781849941617 | £15.99 | PB
320 pages

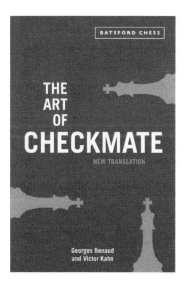

THE ART OF CHECKMATE
Georges Renaud, Victor Kahn
9781849942706 | £15.99 | PB
224 pages

**THE WISEST THINGS
EVER SAID ABOUT CHESS**
Andrew Soltis
9781906388003 | £15.99 | PB
304 pages

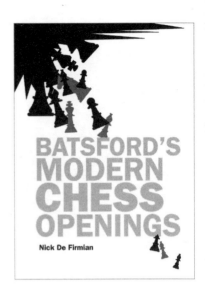

**BATSFORD'S MODERN
CHESS OPENINGS**
Nick De Firmian
9781906388294 | £22.95 | PB
720 pages

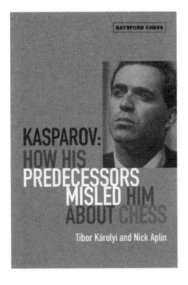

**KASPAROV: HOW HIS
PREDECESSORS MISLED
HIM ABOUT CHESS**
Tibor Karolyi, Nick Aplin
9781906388263 | £14.99 | PB
272 pages

**CRITICAL MOMENTS
IN CHESS**
Paata Gaprindashvili
9781906388652 | £15.99 | PB
288 pages

THE BATSFORD BOOK OF CHESS
Sean Marsh
9781849941648 | £14.99 | HB
208 pages

THE BATSFORD BOOK OF CHESS FOR CHILDREN
Sabrina Chevannes
9781849940696 | £12.99 | HB
128 pages

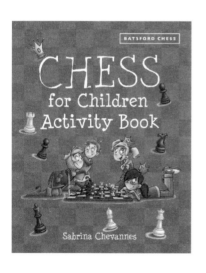

CHESS FOR CHILDREN ACTIVITY BOOK
Sabrina Chevannes
9781849942843 | £9.99 | PB
120 pages